# JOHN
# McCAIN

AMERICAN ★ MAVERICK

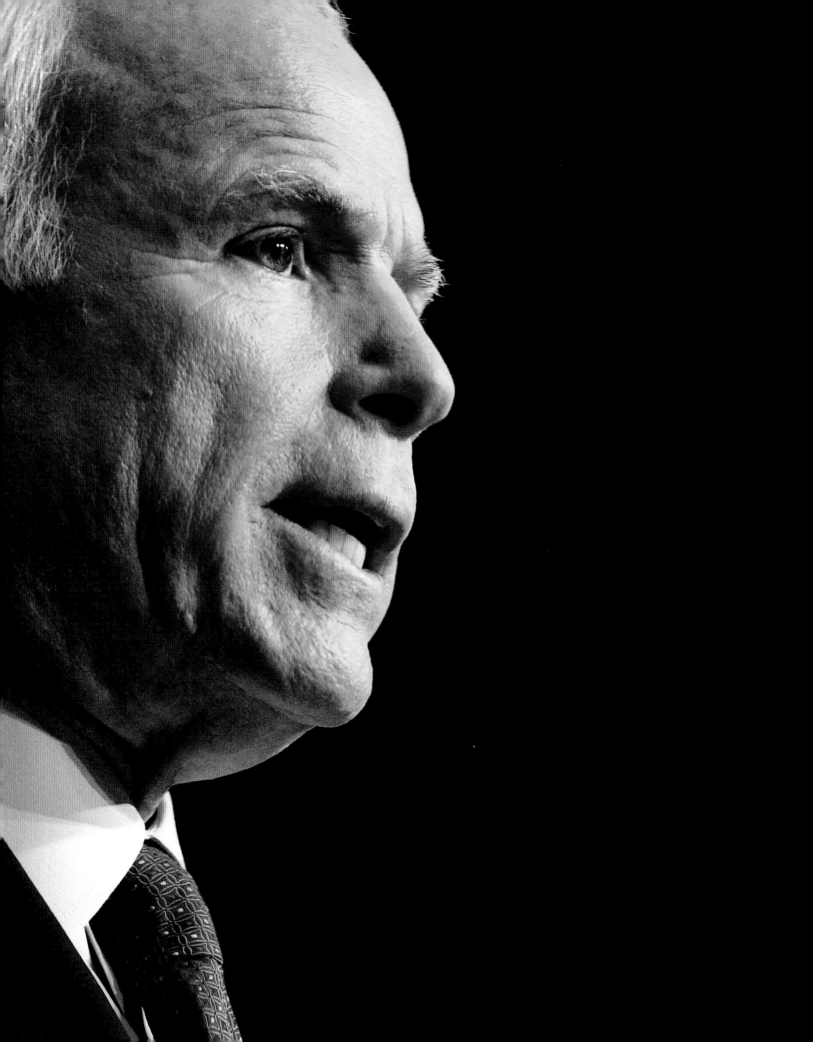

# JOHN McCAIN

## AMERICAN ★ MAVERICK

Foreword by KEN BURNS

Introduction & Text by ELAINE S. POVICH

Photo Editor CHRISTOPHER MEASOM

STERLING
New York

STERLING
New York

An Imprint of Sterling Publishing, Co., Inc.
1166 Avenue of the Americas
New York, NY 10016

ISBN 978-1-4549-3067-9

Distributed in Canada by Sterling Publishing Co., Inc.
c/o Canadian Manda Group, 664 Annette Street
Toronto, Ontario M6S 2C8, Canada
Distributed in the United Kingdom by GMC Distribution Services
Castle Place, 166 High Street, Lewes, East Sussex BN7 1XU, England
Distributed in Australia by NewSouth Books
45 Beach Street, Coogee, NSW 2034, Australia

For information about custom editions, special sales, and premium and corporate purchases, please contact Sterling Special Sales at 800-805-5489 or specialsales@sterlingpublishing.com.

Manufactured in Canada

sterlingpublishing.com

Interior design by Timothy Shaner, NightandDayDesign.biz
Picture Credits — see page 200

# CONTENTS

# FOREWORD

## BY KEN BURNS

The notion of heroism—our ideal of heroism—has clearly been devalued in our omnivorous and essentially amoral media culture, cheapened by a breathless embrace of celebrity over accomplishment, made superficial by our computer age's addiction to the binary—things are either good or bad, red state or blue, white or black or brown, us or them.

We spend far too much time and attention carelessly bestowing heroism on the undeserving or more often melodramatically lamenting our current lack of heroes when we discover *as we always will* that someone in the public sphere is less than perfect—not like our heroes were in the "good old days," we sigh and tell ourselves, though they, of course, never were.

We forget that heroism has never been about perfection. The Greeks, who developed the concept, understood that a hero was a complicated and often strange mix of virtues and vices, and that it was the negotiation—sometimes the war—between the two that actually defined what it means to be a hero. It was that inner struggle between conflicting impulses, not the impossible expectation of perfection, that would fill the songs, stories, and pages of mythology and inspire or repel the very flawed human beings to whom that mythology was directed. Achilles, after all, had his heel and his hubris to go along with his great strengths.

And yet we have always had, and will always have, I believe, a hunger for those we can elevate above the ordinary, individuals of great personal courage and moral integrity, men and women of character and sacrifice and bold action, who help shape the age in which they live, who, despite personal limitations and imperfections, reignite in us a wish to be our best selves.

Fortunately, for those of us blessed to call themselves Americans, we have had a pantheon of heroes to inspire us. From Washington and Franklin and Jefferson, to Lincoln and Frederick Douglass and Harriet Tubman, from Theodore Roosevelt and Franklin and Eleanor Roosevelt, to Jackie Robinson and Cesar Chavez, and many more women and men, we do not lack for models and exemplars of greatness.

At a time when the magnificent tapestry that is our collective strength seems torn and frayed, when ancient animosities seem to pit this group against the other, it is comforting to know we still have among us heroes who help keep the metaphorical wolf from our door.

I would without reservation put John McCain among them. He is, without a doubt, a genuine American hero—complicated, brave, flawed, sacrificing, confounding, inspiring—and above all human. I have had the great privilege of spending time with him on many occasions over the last two-plus decades and each meeting has only reinforced my conviction about his unique and inspirational greatness.

This book will innumerate the myriad acts and accomplishments of this great man. Many will be familiar to most, some new and revelatory, but for me, the key to understanding John McCain, and he will say so himself, is to understand another "hero," another imperfect man, who looms large in McCain's life. His name is Robert Jordan.

Robert Jordan is in fact a fictional character, the protagonist of Ernest Hemingway's great novel about the Spanish Civil War, *For Whom the Bell Tolls.* McCain discovered the novel when he was looking for a book to press a lucky four-leaf clover he had found when he was young. He randomly pulled down from his father's bookshelf Hemingway's masterpiece and started to read. He was hooked, irresistibly drawn to the complicated man at the center of the story.

He was "a man from Montana, a professor," McCain explained to me one fall afternoon, absolutely rapt and lost in the memory of his first encounter with the character who would become his compelling yet contradictory role model. "Robert Jordan was a romantic fatalist. . . . He hears about a struggle many miles away, with a people he did not know, and he decided he would go and fight for what he believed was a just cause, even knowing that that cause was also a flawed one." McCain pauses now, a lump in his throat.

"He was willing to go and fight, to sacrifice for someone else's rights, rights that he would never benefit from, even when he knew [that struggle] was wrong in many ways . . . but he was willing to fight and do whatever he thought he could do for the cause of justice and freedom."

What was it about Jordan that has inspired you in your life? I ask. "Friendship, sacrifice, romance . . . serving a cause greater than yourself. . . . And that is what it's all about. There's nothing more noble than serving a cause greater than yourself."

When he was a prisoner of the North Vietnamese, McCain thought constantly of Jordan. It sustained him, thinking about the chapters, the various characters, the sacrifice his fictional hero makes. He pauses again, composing himself. "My family actually goes back to Charlemagne. . . . One of my ancestors was on General Washington's staff. My grandfather and father were admirals. My great uncles were generals. . . . It's a long history, and, by the way, my sons are in the military," he adds, adroitly and modestly leap-frogging over his own heroic service. "I'm proud of their willingness to serve. And that comes from a long engagement about what's right and what's wrong and about duty and honor and country."

There is some extraordinarily poignant footage taken just after McCain's plane was shot down over Hanoi in October of 1967. The North Vietnamese were so thrilled that they had captured the son of an American admiral they allowed a French journalist to interview him in the hospital. He had just had his broken bones set without even an aspirin for the pain. "I was on a flight over the city of Hanoi," McCain says haltingly, obviously in great pain. ". . . I was bombing and I was hit either by a missile or anti-aircraft fire. . . . I ejected and broke my leg and both my arms and went into a lake; parachuted into a lake. And I was picked up by some North Vietnamese and taken to the hospital, where I almost died. I would just like to tell my wife that I will get well, and I love her and hope to see her soon."

It is an astonishing moment. After that interview, McCain was beaten for not expressing sufficient gratitude to his captors.

John McCain hates this footage; he thinks it shows weakness. But nearly everyone else on the planet clearly sees his bravery, his courage, his loyalty, his love, perhaps even his "romantic fatalism."

And it brings to mind a scene at the end of *For Whom the Bell Tolls* that McCain loves and wishes a listener to understand—this former POW who refused to go home a moment earlier than his fellow captives; a man who would go on to a distinguished, indeed heroic, service in the United States Senate; who would run an unsuccessful but honorable campaign for president; who would courageously speak out for enduring American values, even as his own body was failing him.

In the novel, Robert Jordan and his comrades have successfully blown up a bridge, but he is injured, his leg broken, and the enemy is approaching. He is going to die. Jordan's first thoughts are of the woman he loves and he tries to make sure she will be safe.

But then this *real* American hero, John McCain, a twinkle in his eyes, still a catch in his throat, wants us to remember what his fictional hero said: "The world is a fine place and worth the fighting for and I hate very much to leave it."

—Ken Burns
Walpole, New Hampshire

# INTRODUCTION

## ONE HELL OF A RIDE

John McCain caught lightning in a bottle.

That's how he put the phenomenon that was his campaign for president of the United States in 2000. While ultimately unsuccessful, that mission—scrappy, unpredictable, enlightening, mad, joyful, bewildering—was one hell of a ride.

McCain probably would describe the rest of his life the same way—one hell of a ride.

The "lightning" seems to follow him. Sometimes it will viciously turn on him, as when he was shot down over North Vietnam in 1967, but even then, with a lot of luck, the help of some courageous and unselfish fellow servicemen, and a rare depth of determination, he turned the lightning into light and survived.

He was born to privilege—his father and grandfather were both Navy admirals—but he seemed to fight that privilege the only way he knew how, not by denying it, exactly, but by getting into scrapes in his youth that branded him more a fighter and a firebrand than a future leader. Yet there was always a spark—lightning, if you will—under the wild, cutup youth who became a leader of his country.

*Irrepressible.* That's another word that comes to mind when describing John Sidney McCain III. Only he could talk about the terrifying shootdown of his A-4 Skyhawk airplane as something less than heroic. "I intercepted a Soviet-made surface-to-air missile with my own airplane," he said, with a wry look and chuckle that those who know him have seen often.

Senator John McCain, New York City, 2008.

There's always a twinkle in his eye. Even when spouting off in anger at a fellow senator, unprepared reporter, or hapless congressional witness, there's something there that says, *Listen up, bub, let's not take ourselves too seriously.*

Of course, he is a serious man. He has changed life in the United States with his legislation, his service, his political career, and his example.

But that wasn't always a sure thing. As a young man, he was reckless and arrogant. He violated the rules often—but never so flagrantly that he would jeopardize his ultimate career. He flew jet airplanes competently, but he crashed one into Pensacola Bay, and he took out power lines in Italy by flying too low with another. He ejected from planes a couple of times, too—once when flying to Philadelphia at Christmas to see his first wife, Carol. He was safe, but a cockpit full of gifts were lost.

He survived a devastating fire on USS *Forrestal* in 1967 when a stray spark ignited the flight deck, cooking off bombs and setting fire to jet fuel. What he learned from that experience was that the bombs he was dropping over Vietnam had real tolls on human flesh. It set him to thinking. But the missions continued.

After that fire a chance meeting with the *New York Times*'s legendary reporter R. W. "Johnny" Apple brought him some unscheduled R&R and a chance to see the Vietnam War through a journalist's eyes. The two found they liked each other, despite their different viewpoints.

Throughout his political life, McCain enjoyed jousting with journalists. In the presidential campaign of 2000, McCain often referred to the reporters on his "Straight Talk Express" as "my base," which had more than a grain of truth to it, as he was shut out by many in his own party who were backing George W. Bush in the primaries, and he didn't have enough money to buy a lot of ads. He relied on free media, and the reporters, for their part, relied on his freewheeling comments for a lot of good copy. He also often referred to the reporters as "inmates on a work-release program," which always got a laugh from his audiences and a chuckle from the media members themselves, who knew he was kidding.

Sometimes, McCain would seek out reporters rather than talk to his staff on the bus. He would wander to the back, coffee cup or diet soda in hand (depending on the time of day), and essentially play "ask me anything." He would respond to campaign questions and non-campaign questions. (What's your favorite movie? "*Viva Zapata!*"). It got so bad that some reporters said they could "never" get him to stop talking, even when they needed to write—or sleep. One late evening, fighting Friday rush-hour traffic out of Manhattan bound for Connecticut, he engaged in a country-by-country assessment of the newly independent Soviet Republics with Lars-Erik Nelson, the late columnist for the *New York Daily News*. The rest of the reporters could only gape at the depth of his knowledge of what were then obscure countries.

His camaraderie was not only for reporters. He often showed his genuine love for people. He had trouble firing anyone on his staff, even if they deserved it, usually leaving that distasteful duty to others. He campaigned in high gear—walked fast, talked fast, took pictures fast—trying to corral as many people into his circle as possible.

Maybe the man-in-a-hurry style was a way to continue to make up for the five and a half years he had lost to a prisoner of war camp in North Vietnam. Maybe it stemmed from trying to keep pace with his accomplished relatives. Maybe it was just his way of operating. He never seemed as content as when he was quickly absorbing a topic, tailoring it to his style, and speaking about it soon thereafter. Yet he was sometimes mercurial and testy. He could get angry at something he found distasteful and lash out, but the tempest usually blew over quickly.

His zest for life also manifested itself in his love for women—his friends, his lovers, his wives, his daughters, his mother, and his colleagues. His mother, the estimable Roberta Wright

McCain, who ran off with his father to Tijuana in 1933 for an instant marriage of which her parents disapproved, was the steadying influence in his young life as the Navy family moved around the globe every couple of years.

His first wife, Carol Shepp, was divorced from another Navy man and had two children. She understood the Navy's way of doing things in the 1960s. After they were married in 1965, she was to stay at home while John went to Vietnam. The first few years of their life were happy. They endured his captivity away from each other, but after the war, they could not put the marriage back together. Too much had happened. It was not unusual, but he managed to maintain a cordial relationship with his former wife after his marriage to Cindy Hensley. He is also close to all of his seven children—three with Carol (he adopted Doug and Andrew, her two, and they had a daughter together, Sidney), and four with Cindy: Jack (John Sidney McCain IV), James, Meghan, and Bridget, who was adopted from Bangladesh.

Though Vietnam was the crucible that made him, he refused to let his POW years define him. He was always respectful of prisoners and the POW/MIA movement they inspired, but he wanted more than just to be remembered for surviving. With Cindy, he found a new love and a new passion—politics. He threw himself into that cause—one of the ones he would label as "greater than self-interest"—with unmatched energy.

He survived a lapse of judgment and a minor rebuke from the Senate in the Keating Five scandal. He survived scurrilous attacks on his character, his temperament, his valor, and his family.

The man who was born in the Panama Canal Zone (then a US territory) and who had gone to twenty different schools during the course of his childhood found a home and a political career in Arizona.

He called other people "jerks" or worse, but usually with affection. A wicked sense of humor keeps him real about himself. His response to questions about his age and numerous physical impairments is another often-used line: "I'm older than dirt

and have more scars than Frankenstein." But he has an iron constitution and the ability to be completely refreshed after a catnap on an airplane.

Above it all soars honor—the code by which he has always lived. The worst times of his life were when he felt that honor tarnished, yet they were rare. McCain tries to do what he feels is right. He doesn't always succeed. But he surely has a hell of a good time trying.

If he is remembered for anything, McCain has said, he would like it to be that he "served his country. And I hope, we could add, honorably."

He has done so. And honorably.

The McCain family: (back row from left) Andy, presidential hopeful Senator John McCain, Jack, Cindy, Doug, (front row from left) Jimmy, Bridget, Meghan, and Sidney in New Hampshire on the day of the primary, February 1, 2000.

# PART ONE

# NAVY SON & FAMILY MAN

> "My grandfather was a naval aviator, my father a submariner. They were my first heroes, and earning their respect has been the most lasting ambition of my life."
>
> —John McCain

John McCain's first memory of his father, John Sidney "Jack" McCain Jr., was of him going off to fight a war. It was December 7, 1941, the date that lives "in infamy" for the Japanese attack on Pearl Harbor in World War II. McCain was playing in the front yard of the family's home in New London, Connecticut, where his father, a submariner, was stationed. A car pulled up and a Navy man shouted that the Japanese had bombed Pearl Harbor, Hawaii.

His father left immediately for war and McCain—who was five years old—would not see him much for the next four years.

His life as a child would be directed by the Navy, which had been directing the McCain family for generations. His grandfather John Sidney "Slew" McCain Sr. was an admiral who served in the Pacific theater in World War II.

Young McCain's family moved frequently, forcing Johnny to make a new set of friends over and over. Sometimes he was teased; other times he fought with his fists. He developed a reputation for having a quick temper but also as a fun-loving kid.

He got into trouble at school, but never enough to get tossed out. He developed a tough skin and a gregarious personality. At the Naval Academy, as the son of an admiral, he got special attention and not always of a kind he relished. He was determined to prove he was "one of the boys." His shoes were never shined enough; his shirttail hung out.

(Previous pages) John McCain III (left) with his parents, Roberta and John McCain Jr., at McCain Field, commissioned and named for his grandfather, Admiral John McCain Sr., pictured, July 1961. ◄ John McCain in military dress uniform with his father, ca. 1955.

When he and a group of friends were caught with an impermissible television squirreled away in their bunks, they played the Naval Academy's version of the "rock, paper, scissors" game, called a "shake around," to determine who should take the rap for the infraction. As McCain was just shy of enough demerits to be expelled, his friends agreed to exclude him from the game. Another class-mate took the charge. McCain graduated fifth from the bottom of his class in 1958, a statistic he has often cited as a dose of self-imposed humility.

On his first cruise in 1957 to Rio de Janeiro, he cemented his reputation as a ladies' man by taking up with a Brazilian model, "Maria." They had a whirlwind five-day courtship and a couple of meetings afterward, but the relationship was not lasting. Equally fleeting was his fling with the exotic dancer "Marie, the Flame of Florida," whom he met while stationed at Pensacola, Florida, for flight training.

What was lasting was his marriage to Carol Shepp, who had been previously married to another Navy man and was the mother of two. The two fell in love, got married in 1965, and had their daughter, Sidney, in 1966.

Future senator McCain on his grandfather's lap with his sister, Alexandra, and his parents, John Jr. and Roberta, at the Coco Solo Naval station in the Panama Canal Zone, ca. 1936.

McCain was training for war. He was posted to Jacksonville, Florida, where he joined a squadron that was to go to Vietnam. Carol took the kids to London, where her in-laws, Jack and Roberta, were stationed.

McCain was deployed to Vietnam in 1967, where President Lyndon Johnson had called for an escalation in the bombing. That's what McCain was trained to do. He was in the fight now.

McCain was assigned to the USS *Forrestal*, which, during his tenure, was the site of the horrific 1967 fire in which 135 young Americans died. McCain was only slightly injured, but what he saw there affected him greatly. After a brief recovery period, he was determined to get back into the war and was assigned to the USS *Oriskany*.

On October 21, 1967, one of the largest protests in American history took place in Washington, DC, against the war in Vietnam. The war, however, kept going. Just five days later, McCain climbed into the cockpit of his A-4 Skyhawk for his twenty-third bombing mission. His target was a power plant in Hanoi, an important military target.

The surface-to-air missiles were very thick that day. McCain thought about breaking off the fight and getting away from the missiles, but reckoned that the target was important and that he should try to hit it first. Just as soon as his bombs successfully dove toward the plant, a missile slammed into his plane. He was "killed," in flier parlance.

He pulled the lever for the ejection seat and smashed into the canopy on the way out of the plane, breaking both his arms and his right knee. He landed in Truc Bach Lake, a small pond in the middle of downtown Hanoi.

The citizens pounced on him and began beating him, further aggravating his wounds. He sank to the bottom of the lake several times. Finally, he was pulled from the water by Mai Van On, a clerk at the Ministry of Industry, who prevailed upon the mob to stop beating him.

His next stop was Hoa Lo Prison, the "Hanoi Hilton."

He would not be free again for five and a half years.

"He may have broken every rule
in the book, but he got away
with most of them."

—Dick Thomsen, headmaster
Episcopal High School

◀ With his sister, Alexandra, also known as Sandy, ca. 1938.
▲ From left: Roberta, Joe, John III, John Sr., Sandy, John Jr.,
ca. 1944. ▼ Sophomore John McCain, number 44, on the
Episcopal High School football team, Alexandria, Virginia, 1952.

"I liked the squadron life. We'd be in port for a week, ten days. I was single. I mean, it was wonderful. I was embarrassed to take my paycheck."

—John McCain

▲ Vice Admiral John S. McCain Sr. aboard the USS *Shangri-La*, August 1945. ◄ Vice Admiral John McCain Jr., September 1965.
► Lieutenant John Sidney McCain III, January 1965.

▲ The tragic fire aboard the USS *Forrestal* in the
Tonkin Gulf, July 29, 1967. ▶ John McCain (front
right) with his Navy squadron in 1965.

"In Tokyo Harbor, on the day the Japanese surrendered, they [my father and grandfather] were reunited for the last time. My grandfather would die a few days later. His last words to my father were 'it's an honor to die for your country and your principles.'

—John McCain

▲ With his mother, Roberta, children Jack and Meghan, and wife, Cindy, at the christening of the USS *John S. McCain*, Bath, Maine, September 1992. ▶ McCain's grandfather and father in Tokyo Bay, September 1945.

While McCain titled his first book *Faith of My Fathers*, he has been blessed by having resolute women in his life. His mother, Roberta, a "strong, determined woman," McCain said, raised him and his brother and sister practically alone while his father was deployed around the globe.

His wife, Cindy, similarly was the on-site parent to the four children they had together while he ran and served in the Senate and while he ran for president. "She has raised our four children beautifully," McCain said.

◀ Roberta McCain with her son John on *Meet the Press* in 2007. ▲ With his mother
following his speech at the Republican National Convention, September 4, 2008.
(Following pages) Waiting to be interviewed by MSNBC's Chris Matthews, November 2007.

◀ Jack, Cindy, and Meghan look on as Vice President
George H. W. Bush ceremonially reenacts the swearing-in of
John McCain to the US Senate, January 1987.  ▲ With Bridget,
Meghan, Cindy, and Vice President Dan Quayle during a
swearing-in reenactment, January 1993.

Cindy raised the children in Arizona to give them what she called in a 2008 *People* magazine interview "a well-rounded life." She is chairwoman of Hensley & Co., the family beer distributorship, and is independently wealthy. She founded the American Voluntary Medical Team (1988–1995) and led missions to nations in strife. She also serves on the boards of several nonprofits, including Operation Smile, which sends doctors to countries around the world to correct cleft deformities, like her daughter Bridget once had; the CARE global antipoverty group; and the HALO Trust, which works on landmine removal.

◄ John and Cindy McCain with their children (from left), Meghan, Bridget, Jimmy, and Jack, August 1999. ▲ At home in Phoenix, Arizona, with Jack, Bridget, Meghan, and Jimmy, October 1999.

▲ Outside Elaine's restaurant in New York, 2004. ◀ Cindy with actor and founder
of the Eastern Congo Initiative Ben Affleck at a Senate hearing in Washington, 2014.

▶ Arriving at the Republican National Convention in St. Paul, Minnesota, September 2008.

> "In the absolute end, it's just the two of us. We are our worst critics and our best friends. . . . He advises me on everything, and I advise him on everything."
>
> —Cindy McCain

At the family ranch near Sedona, Arizona, March 9, 2000.

PART TWO

# PRISONER OF WAR

> ## "There is no way I can describe how I felt as I walked toward that US Air Force plane."
>
> —John McCain

The "Hanoi Hilton" bore little resemblance to its namesake.

Initially, McCain was given little medical treatment, little food, and little water. Then his captors figured out who he was. They called him the Prince, since he was the son of an admiral.

Back in London Jack and Roberta heard about the downing of their son's plane. The first news was grim. The presumption was that McCain had not survived, but since that information was not confirmed, his parents went to an already scheduled dinner party. They told no one.

The North Vietnamese decided to let a French film crew record an interview with the badly wounded McCain. His captors wanted him to say that he was getting "humane" treatment. The furthest he would go, even while in unbelievable pain, was "satisfactory." It was enough. His wounds were crudely treated and he was flung into a cell.

With the care of fellow prisoners, giving him what little sustenance he could ingest, he survived. The Vietnamese knew he was the son of a high-ranking Navy

(Previous pages) John McCain exiting a bus upon his release from the prisoner of war camp, March 14, 1973. ◀ John McCain, escorted by PR officer Lieutenant Commander Jay Coupe Jr., heading to Gia Lam Airport in Hanoi for the trip back home, March 14, 1973.
▶ The site of the former Hoa Lo Prison, also known as the "Hanoi Hilton," Vietnam, 2008.

admiral. That was a blessing and a curse. While they didn't really want him to die, they often singled him out for particularly harsh treatment. He endured beatings, was hung by his arms for days, and was taunted as the "crown prince" of the United States.

He was put in solitary confinement for two years. The loquacious McCain, who almost never stopped talking, suddenly had no one to communicate with. It was perhaps harder torture than before. But he discovered that the prisoners had invented a tapping code—a number of taps on the walls between the cells that spelled out letters. It was a cumbersome way to communicate—but it worked. Each conversation started with the old phrase "Shave and a Haircut": *tap, tap-ta tap-tap.* The answer was "two bits," or *tap-tap.*

When McCain's dad was promoted to commander of the Pacific Command in the war, McCain was offered early release. Adhering to the code of conduct requiring the longest-serving prisoner be released first, he refused. The beatings intensified. His captors rebroke his arm, battered his bad knee, and kicked him in the head and ribs. The torture lasted four days. McCain tried to commit suicide, but he was stopped by the guards. He refused to do what his captors wanted. Finally, after enduring unspeakable torture, he agreed to write a statement about how he had committed "black crimes" against the Vietnamese people. "Every man has a breaking point, and I had reached mine," he said later. He was hardest on himself about the incident.

The war dragged on. McCain's time in prison dragged on with it. The treatment began to get a little better, however, and he was allowed contact with other prisoners. They put on plays that they re-created from memory, and McCain led religious services, his Episcopal High School training finally being put to good use.

The bombing of Hanoi in 1972 caused joy among the prisoners, because they knew the United States was upping the pressure to try to end the war. Thousands of miles away, Jack McCain worried every time he ordered a bombing, because he

knew his son was in Hanoi somewhere and could be one of those bombed.

Finally, in 1973, following the Christmas bombings of Hanoi the year before, peace talks between the United States and the North Vietnamese began. One item on the table was release of POWs. On March 14, 1973, McCain was released along with other prisoners. He was not taken out of order, but by his length of time in prison.

There was a restrained celebration among the prisoners as the plane taking them to the Philippines "got its feet wet" over the Tonkin Gulf and into international airspace. McCain's life was forever altered by the experience, but he vowed that it would not be the end to his service.

Hanoi residents pull John McCain out of Truc Bach Lake, October 26, 1967.

" I hit the water and sank to the bottom. I think the lake is about 15 feet deep, maybe 20. I kicked off the bottom. I did not feel any pain at the time, and was able to rise to the surface. I took a breath of air and started sinking again. Of course, I was wearing 50 pounds, at least, of equipment and gear. I went down and managed to kick up to the surface once more. I couldn't understand why I couldn't use my right leg or my arm. I was in a dazed condition. I went up to the top again and sank back down. This time I couldn't get back to the surface. . . . I reached down with my mouth and got the toggle [of my life preserver] between my teeth and inflated the preserver and finally floated to the top. "

—John McCain

(Above and below) Lieutenant Commander and prisoner of war John McCain in a Hanoi hospital in 1967.

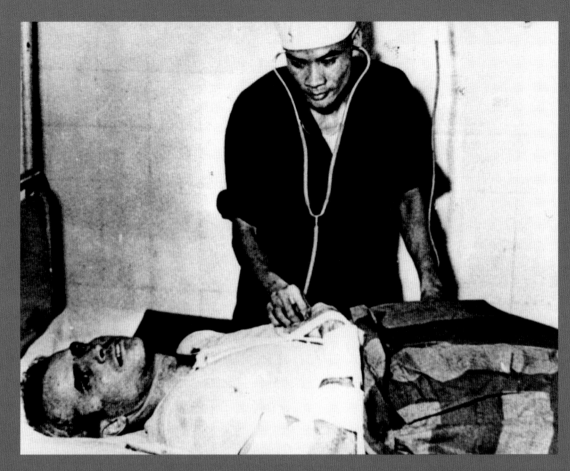

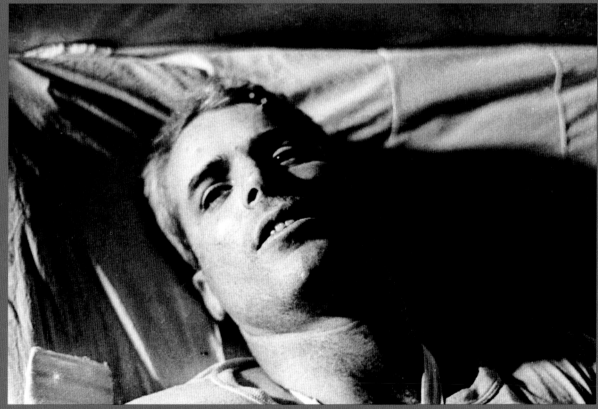

"I knew there was that anti-war element in American society.
I respected their right to do it, so I didn't have any anger about it.
But I had no appreciation of the magnitude of it."

—John McCain

▲ Anti–Vietnam War demonstrators protesting outside the White
House, October 21, 1967. ▶ Some of the 600,000 anti–Vietnam
War protesters marching in Washington, DC, November 15, 1969.

" I fell in love with my country when I was a prisoner in someone else's. I loved it not just for the many comforts of life here. I loved it for its decency; for its faith in the wisdom, justice, and goodness of its people. I loved it because it was not just a place, but an idea, a cause worth fighting for. I was never the same again. I wasn't my own man anymore. I was my country's. "

—John McCain

John McCain during an interview in the United States with *US News & World Report*, after being released from his POW camp, April 1973.

▲ President Nixon chatting with Admiral John S. McCain Jr.,
commander in chief of US forces in the Pacific, February 1969.
▶ President Richard Nixon greeting former prisoner of war John
McCain at a POW dinner reception, May 24, 1973.

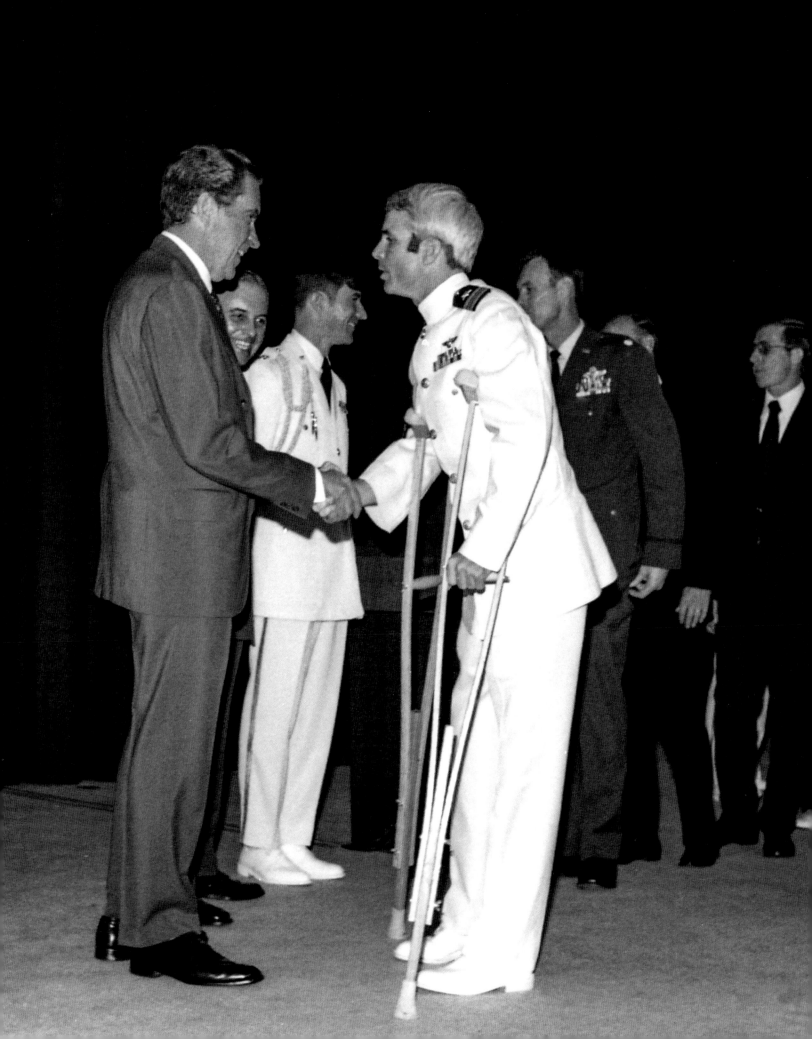

Years after the Vietnam War ended, McCain worked to resolve questions around missing Americans from that war and to normalize trade relations with the former foe. "I'm tired of looking back in anger," he said in *Worth the Fighting For*. He was on a committee in 1993 that concluded there were no more Americans left alive in Vietnam, an attempt to put an end to ongoing reports of "sightings" of Americans there.

◄ John McCain arriving at Clark Air Base in the Philippines, March 14, 1973. ▲ A monument on the shores of Truc Bach Lake in Hanoi commemorating John McCain's capture on October 26, 1967 that reads in part "McCan [sic] . . . the famous air pirate."

"My marriage's collapse was attributable to my own selfishness and immaturity more than it was to Vietnam, and I cannot escape blame by pointing a finger at the war. The blame was entirely mine."

—John McCain

◀ Lieutenant Commander John S. McCain III at Jacksonville Naval Air Station in Florida on March 18, 1973. To the left is his wife, Carol, and son Doug on crutches.
▲ Visiting the Holt orphanage in Saigon, where many of the children of American GIs were cared for, October 30, 1974. ▶ Carol McCain, who was director of the White House Visitors Office from 1981 to 1986, with Ronald Reagan at her farewell party.

▲ Representative McCain on a crowded street in Hanoi during the filming of
a *CBS Reports* special titled "Honor, Duty and a War Called Vietnam," in 1985.
◄ John McCain outside the Army Museum in Hanoi when he was a member of the
Senate Select Committee on servicemen listed as missing in action, 1992. ► On a
tour of Hoa Lo Museum (formerly part of Hoa Lo prison, aka the Hanoi Hilton) in 2009.

> "It doesn't matter to me anymore, Mr. President, who was for the war and who was against the war. I'm tired of looking back in anger. What's important is that we move forward now."
>
> —John McCain to President Clinton arguing for normalizing relations with Vietnam

Chairman of the Senate POW/MIA Committee, Senator John Kerry, working with Senator McCain on unresolved issues at a hearing in 1992.

MR. McCAIN

# SENATOR McCAIN'S ADDRESS TO THE REPUBLICAN NATIONAL CONVENTION

First Union Center, Philadelphia, Pennsylvania
August 1, 2000

I AM GRATEFUL FOR YOUR KINDNESS to a distant runner-up. And I am proud to join you this evening in commending to all Americans the man who now represents your best wishes and mine for the future of our country, my friend, Governor George W. Bush, the next president of the United States.

Tomorrow, we will formally nominate Governor Bush. We do so not for our sake alone. We do not seek his election merely to acquire an advantage over our political opponents or offices for our party faithful. We have a grander purpose than that. When we nominate Governor Bush for president, here in the city where our great nation was born, we invest him with the faith of our Founding Fathers and charge him with the care of the cause they called glorious.

We are blessed to be Americans, not just in times of prosperity, but at all times. We are part of something providential, a great experiment to prove to the world that democracy is not only the most effective form of government, but the only moral government. And through the years, generation after generation of Americans has held fast to the belief that we were meant to transform history.

> We are blessed to be Americans, not just in times of prosperity, but at all times.

On an early December morning, many years ago, I watched my father leave for war. He joined millions of Americans to fight a world war that would decide the fate of humanity. They fought against a cruel and formidable enemy bent on world domination. They fought not just for themselves and their families, not just to preserve the quality of their own lives. They fought for love, for love of an idea—that America stood for something greater than the sum of our individual interests.

From where did the courage come to make the maximum effort in that decisive moment in history? It marched with the sons of a nation that believed deeply in itself, in its history, in the justice of its cause, in its magnificent destiny. Americans went into battle armed against despair with the common conviction that the country that had sent them there was worth their sacrifice. Their families, their schools, their faith, their history, their heroes taught them that the freedom with which they were blessed deserved patriots to defend it.

Many would never come home. But those who did returned with an even deeper civic love. They believed that if America were worth dying for, then surely she was worth living for. They were, as Tocqueville said of Americans, "haunted by visions of what will be." They built an even greater nation than the one they had left their homes to defend, an America that offered more opportunities to more of its people than ever before, an America that began to redress injustices that had been visited on too many of her citizens for too long. They bound up the wounds of war for ally and enemy alike. And when faced with a new, terrible threat to the security and freedom of the world, they fought that, too. As did their sons and daughters. And they prevailed.

Now we stand unsurpassed in our wealth and power. What shall we make of it? Let us take courage from their example, and from the new world they built build a better one.

> Now we stand unsurpassed in our wealth and power. What shall we make of it?

This new century will be an age of untold possibilities for us and for all mankind. Many nations now share our love of liberty and aspire to the ordered progress of democracy. But the world is still home to tyrants, haters, and aggressors hostile to America and our ideals. We are obliged to seize this moment to help build a safer, freer, and more prosperous world, completely free of the tyranny that made the last century such a violent age.

We are strong, confident people. We know that our ideals, our courage, our ingenuity ensure our success. Isolationism and protectionism are fool's errands. We shouldn't build walls to the global success of our interests and values. Walls are for cowards, my friends, not for Americans.

No nation complacent in its greatness will long sustain it. We are an unfinished nation. And we are not a people of half-measures. We who have found shelter beneath the great oak must care for it in our time with as much devotion as had the patriots who preceded us.

This is an extraordinary time to be alive. We are so strong and prosperous that we can scarcely imagine the heights we could ascend if we have the will to make the climb. Yet I think each of us senses that America, for all our prosperity, is in danger of losing the best sense of herself, that there is a purpose to being an American beyond materialism. Cynicism is suffocating the idealism of many Americans, especially among our young. And with cause, for they have lost pride in their government.

Too often those who hold a public trust have failed to set the necessary example. Too often, partisanship seems all consuming. Differences are defined with derision. Too often, we seem to put our personal interests before the national interest, leaving the people's business unattended while we posture, poll, and spin.

> We who have found shelter beneath the great oak must care for it in our time with as much devotion as had the patriots who preceded us.

When the people believe that government no longer embodies our founding ideals, then basic civil consensus will deteriorate as people seek substitutes for the unifying values of patriotism. National pride will not endure the people's contempt for government. And national pride is as indispensable to the happiness of Americans as is our self-respect. Unless we restore the people's sovereignty over government, renew their pride in public service, reform our public institutions to meet the challenges of a new day, and reinvigorate our national purpose, then America's best days will be behind us.

To achieve the necessary changes to the practices and institutions of our democracy we need to be a little less content. We need to get riled up a bit and stand up for the values that made America great. Rally to this new patriotic challenge or lose forever America's extraordinary ability to see around the corner of history.

Americans, enter the public life of your country determined to tell the truth, to put problem solving ahead of partisanship, to defend the national interest against the forces that would divide us. Keep your promise to America, as she has kept her promise to you, and you will know a happiness far more sublime than pleasure.

It is easy to forget in politics where principle ends and selfishness begins. It takes leaders of courage and character to remember the difference. Tomorrow, our party will

Cindy McCain listening to her husband's speech at the 2000 Republican
National Convention in Philadelphia, August 1, 2000.

nominate such a leader. George Bush believes in the greatness of America and the justice of our cause. He believes in the America of the immigrant's dream, the high lantern of freedom and hope to the world. He is proud of America's stature as the world's only superpower, and he accepts the responsibilities along with the blessings that come with that hard-earned distinction. He knows well that there is no safe alternative to American leadership. And he will not squander this unique moment in history by allowing America to retreat behind empty threats, false promises, and uncertain diplomacy. He will confidently defend our interests and values wherever they are threatened.

I say to all Americans—Republican, Democrat or Independent—if you believe America deserves leaders with a purpose more ennobling than expediency and opportunism, then vote for Governor Bush. If you believe patriotism is more than a sound bite and public service should be more than a photo op, then vote for Governor Bush.

My friend Governor Bush believes in an America that is so much more than the sum of its divided parts. He wants to give you back a government that serves all the people no matter the circumstances of their birth. And he wants to lead a Republican Party that is as big as the country we serve. He wants nothing to divide us into separate nations. Not our color. Not our race. Not our wealth. Not our religion. Not our politics. He wants us to live for America, as one nation, and together profess the American creed of self-evident truths.

I support him. I am grateful to him. And I am proud of him.

He is a good man from a good family that has, in good times and bad, dedicated themselves to America. Many years ago, the governor's father served in the Pacific, with

John McCain congratulating the Republican presidential candidate George W. Bush at the end of the Republican National Convention, August 3, 2000.

distinction, under the command of my grandfather. Now it is my turn to serve under the son of my grandfather's brave subordinate. I am proud to do so, for I know that by supporting George W. Bush I serve my country well.

My grandfather was an aviator; my father a submariner. They gave their lives to their country. In Tokyo Harbor, on the day the Japanese surrendered, they were reunited for the last time. My grandfather would die a few days later. His last words to my father were "it's an honor to die for your country and your principles." I have been an imperfect servant of my country for over forty years, and my many mistakes rightly humble me. But I am their son . . . and they taught me to love my country, and that has made all the difference, my friends, all the difference in the world.

I am so grateful to have seen America rise to such prominence. But America's greatness is a quest without end, the object beyond the horizon. And it is an inescapable and bittersweet irony of life, that the older we are the more distant the horizon becomes. I will not see what is over America's horizon. The years that remain are not too few, I trust, but the immortality that was the aspiration of my youth has, like all the treasures of youth, quietly slipped away.

> I have faith that just beyond the distant horizon live a people who gratefully accept the obligation of their freedom to make of their power and wealth a civilization for the ages.

But I have faith. I have faith in you. I have faith in your patriotism, in your passion to build upon the accomplishments of our storied past. I have faith that people who are free to act in their own interests will perceive their interests in an enlightened way and live as one nation, in a kinship of ideals, served by a government that kindles the pride of every one of you. I have faith that just beyond the distant horizon live a people who gratefully accept the obligation of their freedom to make of their power and wealth a civilization for the ages—a civilization in which all people share in the promise of freedom.

I have such faith in you, my fellow Americans. And I am haunted by the vision of what will be.

PART THREE

# STRAIGHT TALK
# EXPRESS

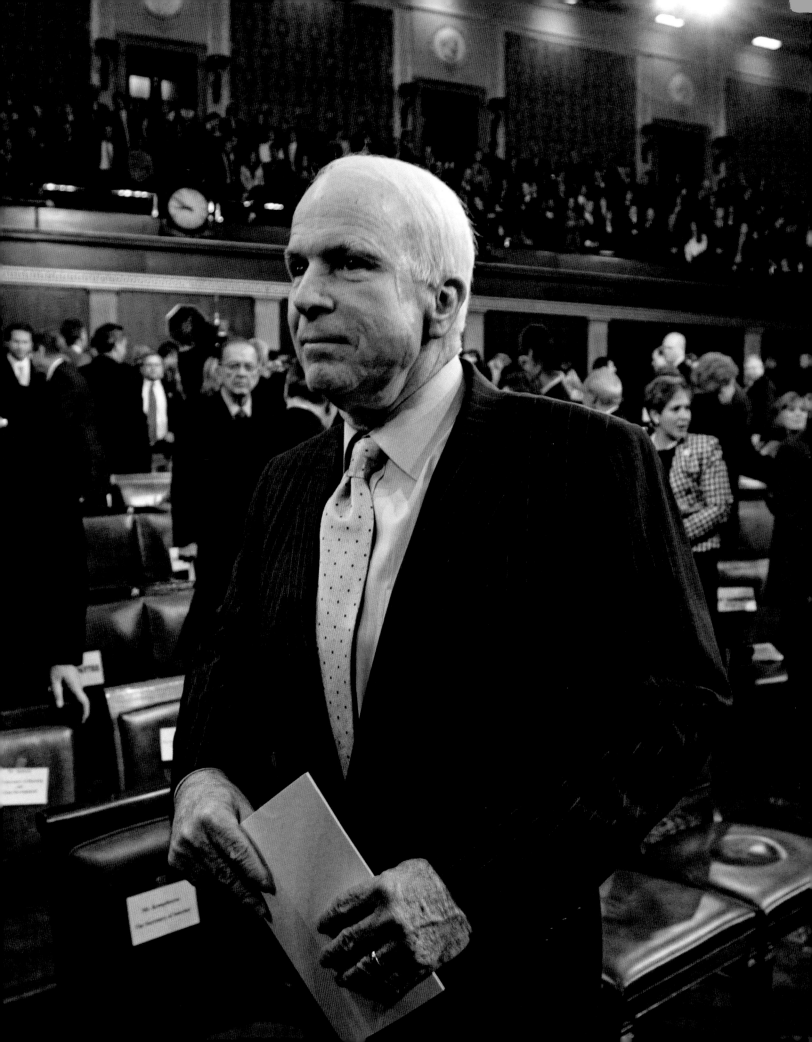

> ## "Make no mistake, my service here is the most important job I've had in my life."
>
> —John McCain

Getting healthy and back into flight status was McCain's goal. Surgeries and a long period of rehabilitation made it possible for him to fly again, at least for a time, but he knew he would never be in combat again nor rise to the level achieved by his famous forebears. After a stint as the Navy's liaison to the US Senate, he made the difficult decision to leave the Navy. The hardest part was telling his dad, who tried to talk him out of it. But he had decided.

While he returned seamlessly to the Navy after imprisonment, the same could not be said for his personal life. After an initial happy reunion with Carol, the two found they had grown apart during the separation. He said in 2008 that his "greatest moral failure" was the dissolution of his marriage.

"My marriage's collapse was attributable to my own selfishness and immaturity more than it was to Vietnam, and I cannot escape blame by pointing a finger at the war. The blame was entirely mine," he wrote in *Worth the Fighting For* (2002).

While he and Carol were separated he met Cindy Hensley. The two fell for each other, and—in what later became a running joke between them—each lied about the seventeen-year difference in their ages: McCain made himself a bit younger, and Cindy made herself a bit older. Despite starting the relationship with a couple of lies, it flourished, and they were married in 1980, shortly after John and Carol divorced.

(Previous pages) Confetti falls at a town hall meeting with voters in Peterborough, New Hampshire, January 30, 2000. ◀ At President George W. Bush's State of the Union address on Capitol Hill, January 23, 2007.

Being the Navy's liaison to the Senate had sparked his interest in politics, but he was unsure of how to pursue that idea. His new wife provided both a new life and the way to a new career. They settled in Phoenix, her hometown, and McCain went to work for the family beer distributorship. But his fame as the most recognizable former POW and his public relations job helped him become more widely known around town, and business and civic leaders began to see him as a charismatic and popular speaker.

Then, fate intervened. A House seat opened up in 1982. John and Cindy scrambled to buy a home in the district to establish residency. But McCain, a newcomer to Arizona, could not shake the label of "carpetbagger." Then one night, he settled the issue.

Answering the carpetbagger question once again, he snapped: "Listen, pal. I spent twenty-two years in the Navy. My father was in the Navy. My grandfather was in the Navy. We in the military service tend to move a lot. We have to live in all parts of the country, all parts of the world. I wish I could have had the luxury, like you, of growing up and living and spending my entire life in a nice place like the First District of Arizona, but I was doing different things. As a matter of fact, the place I lived the longest in my life was Hanoi."

Boom. Controversy over. Race over. He won the House seat.

McCain served in the House until 1986, when he ran for and won the Senate seat once held by the fiery conservative Barry Goldwater. He was back in Washington but in the Senate this time, where he immediately felt comfortable. Instead of carrying senators' bags, however, this time he was making laws.

McCain concentrated on foreign affairs and military issues in the Senate. He had a good reputation, but in 1989 he was caught up in a painful episode that would leave him chastened but determined—the Keating Five scandal, in which five senators were investigated for unethically trying to help financier (and campaign donor) Charles Keating with what turned out to be banking improprieties. In the end McCain got a slap on the wrist (he was cleared of impropriety in 1991—the Senate Ethics Committee found his actions were not improper nor attended with gross negligence—but he was chastised by the committee for "poor judgment"). But it affected him profoundly. He once told former senator Warren Rudman that the episode was worse, in some ways, than being in a North Vietnamese prison. It was all about his honor, and to have that besmirched was crushing to him.

But it led him to his next major mission—getting big money out of politics. The McCain-Feingold Act revamped campaign financing, and because he went up against leaders of his own party, it also cemented his reputation as a maverick.

It was that reputation that fueled his campaign for president in 2000—on a shoestring budget, toting reporters around New Hampshire, the first primary state, on a bus called the "Straight Talk Express." He won the New Hampshire primary, but was crushed by George W. Bush in later primaries and left the race.

But his appetite had been whetted. In 2008, he was better funded and more experienced, and using a much more traditional approach than in 2000, he won the Republican nomination. At his triumphant convention in St. Paul, Minnesota, he stunned both the party and the country by selecting Alaska governor Sarah Palin as his running mate, the first female Republican vice presidential candidate. The choice shook up the race, and for a time McCain was riding high. But Palin turned out to be a problematic choice, unfamiliar with national issues and prone to verbal miscues. McCain took both credit and blame for his pick. Ultimately, he lost the race to Barack Obama, the first African American president.

He was gracious in the loss, and while he may have disagreed with President Obama, he rejected personal attacks made on the president.

"I wish Godspeed to the man who was my former opponent and will be my president," McCain said.

▼ Presidential hopeful Senator John McCain with his wife, Cindy, as the campaign kicks off in Greenville, South Carolina, on July 31, 1999. ◄ With supporters at the campus of Arizona State University before the GOP debate, November 1999. ▲ At the Pacific Design Center in Los Angeles on Super Tuesday, March 8, 2000. (Following pages) Campaigning at an American Legion Hall in Seneca, South Carolina, July 1999.

◄ In front of a Dartmouth College fraternity house in Hanover, New Hampshire, January 31, 2000. ▲ With reporters aboard the Straight Talk Express in South Carolina, January 2000. ▶ From left: publisher Steve Forbes, former diplomat Alan Keyes, Texas governor George W. Bush, Utah senator Orrin Hatch, Arizona senator John McCain, and activist Gary Bauer at a debate in Des Moines, Iowa, December 13, 1999.

◀ Lunch in Anderson, South Carolina, while campaigning, July 1999.

▲ In his motel room in New Hampshire in November 1999.

> " I ribbed aides and supporters, identifying them as Spanish-American War veterans and work release parolees. I was, in short having a hell of a lot of fun, which, as superficial as it sounds, was one of the purposes of the campaign. "
>
> —John McCain

January 7, 2000 in Columbia, South Carolina.
(Following pages) The McCain family on the campaign
trail in Keene, New Hampshire, January 2000.
From left: Cindy, Bridget, Jack, Jimmy, and Meghan.

◄ Advisor John Weaver (left) and Senator Russ Feingold with John
and Cindy McCain. ▲ John McCain calling George W. Bush to
concede following his Super Tuesday losses, March 8, 2000.

## STATEMENT BY SENATOR JOHN MCCAIN REGARDING THE SUSPENSION OF HIS PRESIDENTIAL CAMPAIGN

Sedona, Arizona
March 9, 2000

WE KNEW WHEN WE BEGAN this campaign that ours was a difficult challenge. Last Tuesday, that challenge became considerably more difficult as a majority of Republican voters made clear their preference for president is Governor Bush. I respect their decision and I am truly grateful for the distinct privilege of even being considered for the highest office in this, the greatest nation in the history of mankind.

Therefore, I announce today, on this fine Arizona morning and in this beautiful place, that I am no longer an active candidate for my party's nomination for president. I congratulate Governor Bush and wish him and his family well. He may very well become the next president of the United States. That is an honor accorded to very few, and is such a great responsibility that he deserves the best wishes of every American. He certainly has mine.

I'm suspending my campaign so that Cindy and I can take some time to reflect on our recent experiences and determine how we can best continue to serve the country and help bring about the changes to the practices and the institutions of our great democracy that are the purpose of our campaign. For we believe these changes are essential to ensuring the continued success of the American experiment and keeping America in this new century as bright a beacon of hope for mankind as it was in the last.

I hoped our campaign would be a force for change in the Republican Party. And I believe we have, indeed, set a course that will ultimately prevail in making our party as big as the country we serve. Millions of Americans have rallied to our banner. And their support not just honors me, but has ignited the cause of reform, a cause far greater and more important than the ambitions of any single candidate.

I love my party. It is my home. Ours is the party of Lincoln, Roosevelt, and Reagan. That's good company for any American to keep. And it is a distinct privilege to serve the same cause that those great Americans dedicated their lives to. But I'm also dedicated to the necessary cause of reform, and I will never walk away from a fight for what I know is right and just for our country. As I said throughout the campaign, what is good for my country is good for my party. Should our party ever abandon this principle, the American people will rightly abandon us. And we will surely slip into the mist of history deserving the allegiance of none.

So I will take our crusade back to the United States Senate. And I will keep fighting to save the government, to give the government back to the people, to keep our promises to young and old alike by paying our debts, saving Social Security and Medicare, and reforming a tax code that benefits the powerful few at the expense of many. And with your help, my fellow Americans, we will keep trying to force open doors where there are walls to your full participation in the great enterprises of our democracy, be they walls of cynicism or intolerance or walls raised by self-interested elite who would exclude your voice from the highest councils of our government.

I want to take a final moment to speak to all those who joined our party to support our campaign, many of whom voted in this election for the first time. Thank you. Thank you from the bottom of my heart. Your support means more to me than I can ever say. But I ask from you one last promise: Promise me that you will never give up, that you will continue your service in the worthy cause of revitalizing our democracy. Our crusade will never accomplish all its goals if your voices fall silent in our national debate. You are, and always will be, the best thing about this campaign and the best hope for our country's future success. Stay in this fight with us. We need your service as much as ever.

Millions of Americans over the years have, by their example, showed us that America and her causes are worth dying for. Surely, she is worth living for. That is what I ask of all Americans who found in our campaign an expression for their patriotism. I am so proud of you and so grateful for your company.

I have been in my country's service since I was seventeen years old. I neither know nor want any other life, for I can find no greater honor than service. You served your country in this campaign by fighting for the causes that will sustain America's greatness. Keep fighting, my friends, keep fighting; America needs you.

Thank you, my friends. Thank you so much for helping me remember what it means to be a public servant in this the most blessed and most important nation on earth. It has been the greatest privilege of my life.

"Therefore, I announce today, on this fine Arizona morning and in this beautiful place, that I am no longer an active candidate for my party's nomination for president."

—John McCain

Senator John McCain announcing his withdrawal from the presidential race at a press conference overlooking the Sedona valley on March 9, 2000.

> " When the pundits declared us finished, I told them I'm going to New Hampshire where the voters don't let you make their decision for them. And when they asked, 'How are you going to do it? You're down in the polls. You don't have the money.' I answered, 'I'm going to New Hampshire, and I'm going to tell people the truth.' "

—John McCain

(Previous pages) After speaking at a house party in Tilton, New Hampshire, on New Year's Day 2008. ▶ Celebrating the win in New Hampshire, January 8, 2008.

# JOHN MCCAIN'S NEW HAMPSHIRE PRIMARY SPEECH

Ballroom of the Crowne Plaza Hotel, Nashua, New Hampshire
January 8, 2008

FIRST, I'D LIKE TO THANK my wife, Cindy, and my seven children, and all of our campaign team, who did such a wonderful job. And I'm very grateful.

My friends, you know, I'm past the age when I can claim the noun "kid," no matter what adjective precedes it. But tonight, we sure showed them what a comeback looks like.

When the pundits declared us finished, I told them I'm going to New Hampshire where the voters don't let you make their decision for them. And when they asked, "How are you going to do it? You're down in the polls. You don't have the money." I answered, "I'm going to New Hampshire, and I'm going to tell people the truth." We came back here to this wonderful state we've come to trust and love. And we had just one strategy: to tell you what I believe.

I didn't just tell you what the polls said you wanted to hear. I didn't tell you what I knew to be false. I didn't try to spin you. I just talked to the people of New Hampshire. I talked about the country we love, the many challenges we face together, and the great promise that is ours to achieve.

The work that awaits us in this hour on our watch, to defend our country from its enemies, to advance the ideals that are our greatest strengths, to increase the prosperity and opportunities of all Americans, and to make in our time, as each preceding American generation has, another better world than the one we inherited.

I talked to the people of New Hampshire. I reasoned with you. I listened to you. I answered you. Sometimes, I argued with you. But I always told you the truth as best I can see the truth. And you did me the great honor of listening. Thank you, New Hampshire, from the bottom of my heart. I'm grateful and humbled and more certain than ever before that, before I can win your vote, I must win your respect. And I must do that by being honest with you and then put my trust in your fairness and good judgment.

> . . . tonight, we sure showed them what a comeback looks like.

In his suite at the Crowne Plaza Hotel with his daughter Meghan after hearing that he was the projected winner of the New Hampshire primary, January 8, 2008.

Tonight, we have taken a step, but only the first step, toward repairing the broken politics of the past and restoring the trust of the American people in their government.

The people of New Hampshire have told us again that they do not send us to Washington to serve our self-interest, but to serve theirs.

They don't send us to fight each other for our own political ambitions, but to fight together our real enemies. They don't send us to Washington to stroke our egos, to keep this beautiful, bountiful, blessed country safe, prosperous, and proud.

**I seek the nomination of a party that believes in the strength, industry, and goodness of the American people.**

They don't send us to Washington to take more of their money and waste it on things that add not an ounce to America's strength and prosperity, that don't help a single family realize the dreams we all dream for our children, that don't help a single displaced worker find a new job and the security and dignity it assures them, that won't keep the promise we make to young workers that the retirement they have begun to invest in will be there for them when they need it.

They don't send us to Washington to do their job, but to do ours.

My friends, I didn't go to Washington to go along to get along or to play it safe to serve my own interests. I went there to serve my country. And that, my friends, is just what I intend to do if I am so privileged to be elected your president.

I seek the nomination of a party that believes in the strength, industry, and goodness of the American people. We don't believe that government has all the answers, but that it should respect the rights, property, and opportunities of the people to whom we are accountable.

We don't believe in growing the size of government to make it easier to serve our own ambitions. But what government is expected to do it must do with competence, resolve, and wisdom.

In recent years, we have lost the trust of the people who share our principles but doubt our own allegiance to them.

I seek the nomination of our party to restore that trust, to return our party to the principles that have never failed Americans, the party of fiscal discipline, low taxes, enduring values, a strong and capable defense that encourages the enterprise and ingenuity of individuals, businesses, and families who know best how to advance America's economy and secure the dreams that have made us the greatest nation in history.

The work that we face in our time is great, but our opportunities greater still. In a time of war and the terrible sacrifices it entails, the promise of a better future is not always clear. But I promise you, my friends, we face no enemy, no matter how cruel, and no challenge, no matter how daunting, greater than the courage, patriotism, and determination of Americans. We are the makers of history, not its victims.

And as we confront this enemy, the people privileged to serve in public office should not evade our mutual responsibility to defeat them because we are more concerned with personal or partisan ambition. Whatever the differences between us, so much more should unite us, and nothing should unite us more closely than the imperative of defeating an enemy who despises us, our values, and modernity itself.

We must all pull together in this critical hour and proclaim that the history of the world will not be determined by this unpardonable foe but by the aspirations, ideals, faith, and the courage of free people in this great, historic task. We will never surrender. They will.

The results of the other party's primary is uncertain at this time tonight, but I want to congratulate all the campaigns in both parties. I salute the supporters of all the candidates who worked so hard to achieve a success tonight and who believe so passionately in the promise of their candidate.

And I want to assure them that though I did not have their support, and though we may disagree from time to time on how to best advance America's interests and ideals, they have my genuine respect, for they have worked for a cause they believe is good for the country we all love, a cause greater than their self-interest.

The work that we face in our time is great, but our opportunities greater still.

My friends, I learned long ago that serving only one's self is a petty and unsatisfying ambition. But serve a cause greater than self-interest and you will know a happiness far more sublime than the fleeting pleasure of fame and fortune. For me, that greater cause has always been my country, which I have served imperfectly for many years, but have loved without any reservation every day of my life.

And however this campaign turns out—and I am more confident tonight that it will turn out much better than once expected—I am grateful beyond expression for the prospect that I might serve her a little while longer.

That gratitude imposes on me the responsibility to do nothing in this campaign that would make our country's problems harder to solve or that would cause Americans to despair that a candidate for the highest office in the land would think so little of the honor that he would put his own interests before theirs. I take that responsibility as my most solemn trust.

So, my friends, we celebrate one victory tonight and leave for Michigan tomorrow to win another. But let us remember that our purpose is not ours alone. Our success is not an end in itself. America is our cause, yesterday, today, and tomorrow. Her greatness is our hope; her strength is our protection; her ideals, our greatest treasure; her prosperity, the promise we keep to our children; her goodness, the hope of mankind.

That is the cause of our campaign and the platform of my party. And I will stay true to it, so help me God.

Thank you, New Hampshire. Thank you, my friends. And God bless you as you have blessed me. Enjoy this. You have earned it more than me. Tomorrow, we begin again.

Thank you.

For me, that greater cause has always been my country, which I have served imperfectly for many years, but have loved without any reservation every day of my life.

Smiles all around as McCain is projected to win the New Hampshire primary, January 8, 2008.

◀ Shaking hands with (and buying pastries from) Carolyn Sharpe in Tiffin, Ohio, October 2008. ▲ At a campaign rally in Columbus, Ohio, with Cindy and Meghan McCain, California governor Arnold Schwarzenegger, Senator Lindsey Graham, and country music artist Hank Williams Jr. less than a week before the US presidential election.

◀ Denver, 2008.  ▲ A selfie with a supporter in Manchester, New Hampshire, September, 2008.
▶ A campaign stop at a coffee shop in Meredith, New Hampshire, November, 2007.

"I am proud of my record, and I am proud of reaching across the aisle and getting things done. That's what the American people want us to do."

—John McCain

▲ Candidate McCain with former congressman Rob Portman onboard Straight Talk Air in 2008. ◀ At the 2008 Outagamie County GOP Lincoln Day Dinner in Appleton, Wisconsin. ▶ John McCain and Mitt Romney as the GOP presidential debate at the Ronald Reagan Presidential Library gets under way on January 30, 2008.

(Previous pages) Outside the Straight Talk Express on primary day in Nashua, New Hampshire, January 8, 2008. ◀ Shaking hands with Dorothy Robie during a campaign stop at Robie's General Store in Hooksett, New Hampshire, October 14, 2007. ▲ Boarding his plane at Dulles Airport, February 2008.

"There were many people who
said, 'McCain's political chances or
opportunities or career is over.' I said
that's fine, that's fine—I would much rather
lose a political campaign than lose a war."

—John McCain

Speaking at Faneuil Hall in Boston, February 4, 2008.
(Following pages) Stopping at the American Legion Hall in
Waterloo, Iowa, during his "No Surrender" tour in 2007.

105

"Reporters became my constant companions and I, theirs. We leased a bus and christened it the Straight Talk Express. I took all questions, ducked nothing, and talked for hours on end."

—John McCain

▲ Senator John McCain with the press on the Straight Talk Express, January 2008. ▶ Campaigning at Morse Sporting Goods in Hillsborough, New Hampshire, November 2007.

▲ Senator and Mrs. John McCain greet supporters after his one-hundredth town hall meeting in Peterborough, New Hampshire, January 2008.
▶ Cindy McCain wiping lipstick off the candidate's face after kissing him during a town hall–style meeting in Denver, July 2008. (Following pages) In Iowa on the forty-first anniversary of his capture in North Vietnam and less than two weeks before the presidential election, October 2008.

◀ Campaigning in West Palm Beach, Florida, January 2008. ▲ Cheers
for Republican presidential nominee Senator John McCain during a
campaign rally at the University of Northern Iowa, October 26, 2008.

"It's a long way from the fear, and pain, and squalor of a six-by-four cell in Hanoi to the Oval Office. But if Senator McCain is elected president, that is the journey he will have made. It's the journey of an upright and honorable man. . . . He would bring the compassion that comes from having once been powerless, the wisdom that comes even to the captives by the grace of God, the special confidence of those who have seen evil and have seen how evil is overcome."

—Sarah Palin

Vice presidential candidate Sarah Palin is joined by presidential candidate John McCain and her daughter Piper at the end of her speech at the Republican National Convention in St. Paul, Minnesota, September 3, 2008.

"I hit a home run with John McCain! I got the most
marvelous husband and friend and confidant—a
source of strength and inspiration—and also the
best father you could ever imagine."

—Cindy McCain

◀ The presidential candidate's family at the Republican National
Convention on September 4, 2008. From left: Andrew, Meghan, Jimmy,
Cindy, Jack, Douglas, Bridget, and Sidney. ▲ The Republican presidential
nominee John McCain and his wife, Cindy, wave to the cheering crowd.

# PRESIDENTIAL NOMINATION ACCEPTANCE SPEECH [abridged]

Republican National Convention St. Paul, Minnesota
Thursday, September 4, 2008

TONIGHT, I HAVE A PRIVILEGE given few Americans: the privilege of accepting our party's nomination for president of the United States. And I accept it with gratitude, humility, and confidence.

In my life, no success has come without a good fight, and this nomination wasn't any different. That's a tribute to the candidates who opposed me and their supporters. They're leaders of great ability who love our country and wish to lead it to better days. Their support is an honor that I won't forget.

I'm grateful to the president of the United States for leading us in these dark days following the worst attack on American soil in our history . . .

As always, I'm indebted to my wife, Cindy, and my seven children. You know, the pleasures of family life can seem like a brief holiday from the crowded calendar of our nation's business. But I have treasured them all the more and can't imagine a life without the happiness that you've given me.

> The pleasures of family life can seem like a brief holiday from the crowded calendar of our nation's business.

You know, Cindy said a lot of nice things about me tonight. But, in truth, she's more my inspiration than I am hers. Her concern for those less blessed than we are—victims of landmines, children born in poverty, with birth defects—shows the measure of her humanity. And I know that she will make a great First Lady.

My friends, when I was growing up, my father was often at sea, and the job of raising my brother, sister, and me would fall to my mother alone. Roberta McCain gave us her love of life, her deep interest in the world, her strength, and her belief that we're all meant to use our opportunities to make ourselves useful to our country. I wouldn't be here tonight but for the strength of her character. And she doesn't want me to say this, but she's ninety-six years young.

Addressing the Republican National Convention,
St. Paul, Minnesota, September 4, 2008.

My heartfelt thanks to all of you who helped me win this nomination and stood by me when the odds were long. I won't let you down.

To Americans who have yet to decide who to vote for, thank you for your consideration and the opportunity to win your trust. I intend to earn it.

And, finally, a word to Senator Obama and his supporters. We'll go at it over the next two months—you know that's the nature of this business—and there are big differences between us. But you have my respect and my admiration. Despite our differences, much more unites us than divides us. We are fellow Americans, and that's an association that means more to me than any other.

We're dedicated to the proposition that all people are created equal and endowed by our creator with inalienable rights. No country ever had a greater cause than that. And I wouldn't be an American worthy of the name if I didn't honor Senator Obama and his supporters for their achievement.

But let there be no doubt, my friends: We're going to win this election. And after we've won, we're going to reach out our hand to any willing patriot, make this government start working for you again, and get this country back on the road to prosperity and peace. . . .

And I've found just the right partner to help me shake up Washington, Governor Sarah Palin of the great state of Alaska. . . .

She's tackled tough problems, like energy independence and corruption. She's balanced a budget, cut taxes, and she's taken on the special interests. She's reached across the aisle and asked Republicans, Democrats, and Independents to serve in her administration. She's the wonderful mother of five children. She's helped run a small business. She's worked with her hands and knows what it's like to worry about mortgage payments, and healthcare, and the cost of gasoline and groceries. . . . She stands up for what's right, and she doesn't let anyone tell her to sit down. I'm very proud to have introduced our next vice president to the country, but I can't wait until I introduce her to Washington. . . .

You well know I've been called a maverick, someone who marches to the beat of his own drum. Sometimes it's meant as a compliment; sometimes it's not. What it really means is I

We'll go at it over the next two months—you know that's the nature of this business. . . . But . . . much more unites us than divides us.

understand who I work for. I don't work for a party. I don't work for a special interest. I don't work for myself. I work for you.

I've fought corruption, and it didn't matter if the culprits were Democrats or Republicans. . . . I've fought the big spenders in both parties, who waste your money on things you neither need nor want. . . .

We're not going to allow that while you struggle to buy groceries, fill your gas tank, and make your mortgage payment. I've fought to get million-dollar checks out of our elections. I've fought lobbyists who stole from Indian tribes. I've fought crooked deals in the Pentagon. I've fought tobacco companies and trial lawyers, drug companies and union bosses. I've fought for the right strategy and more troops in Iraq when it wasn't the popular thing to do.

And when the pundits said my campaign was finished, I said I'd rather lose an election than see my country lose a war. . . .

I don't mind a good fight. For reasons known only to God, I've had quite a few tough ones in my life. But I learned an important lesson along the way: In the end, it matters less that you can fight. What you fight for is the real test. . . .

I fight to restore the pride and principles of our party. We were elected to change Washington, and we let Washington change us.

We lost the trust of the American people when some Republicans gave in to the temptations of corruption. We lost their trust when rather than reform government, both parties made it bigger. We lost their trust when instead of freeing ourselves from a dangerous dependence on foreign oil, both parties—and Senator Obama—passed another corporate welfare bill for oil companies. We lost their trust when we valued our power over our principles.

We're going to change that. . . . The party of Lincoln, Roosevelt, and Reagan is going to get back to basics.

In this country, we believe everyone has something to contribute and deserves the opportunity to reach their God-given potential, from the boy whose descendants arrived

You well know I've been called a maverick, someone who marches to the beat of his own drum. Sometimes it's meant as a compliment; sometimes it's not.

on the *Mayflower* to the Latina daughter of migrant workers. We're all God's children, and we're all Americans.

We believe in low taxes, spending discipline, and open markets. We believe in rewarding hard work and risk takers and letting people keep the fruits of their labor.

We believe in a strong defense, work, faith, service, a culture of life, personal responsibility, the rule of law, and judges who dispense justice impartially and don't legislate from the bench.

We believe in the values of families, neighborhoods, and communities. We believe in a government that unleashes the creativity and initiative of Americans, government that doesn't make your choices for you, but works to make sure you have more choices to make for yourself. . . .

Today the prospect of a better world remains within our reach. But we must see the threats to peace and liberty in our time clearly and face them as Americans before us did: with confidence, wisdom, and resolve. . . .

We face many dangerous threats in this dangerous world, but I'm not afraid of them. I'm prepared for them. I know how the military works, what it can do, what it can do better, and what it shouldn't do. I know how the world works. I know the good and the evil in it. I know how to work with leaders who share our dreams of a freer, safer and more prosperous world, and how to stand up to those who don't. I know how to secure the peace.

My friends, when I was five years old, a car pulled up in front of our house. A Navy officer rolled down the window and shouted at my father that the Japanese had bombed Pearl Harbor. I rarely saw my father again for four years. My grandfather came home from that same war exhausted from the burdens he had borne and died the next day. In Vietnam, where I formed the closest friendships of my life, some of those friends never came home with me.

I hate war. It's terrible beyond imagination.

I'm running for president to keep the country I love safe and prevent other families from risking their loved ones in war as my family has. . . .

> I don't work for a party. I don't work for a special interest. I don't work for myself. I work for you.

In America, we change things that need to be changed. Each generation makes its contribution to our greatness. The work that is ours to do is plainly before us; we don't need to search for it. We need to change the way government does almost everything: from the way we protect our security to the way we compete in the world economy; from the way we respond to disasters to the way we fuel our transportation network; from the way we train our workers to the way we educate our children. . . .

This amazing country can do anything we put our minds to. I'll ask Democrats and Independents to serve with me. . . . We're going to finally start getting things done for the people who are counting on us, and I won't care who gets the credit.

My friends, I've been an imperfect servant of my country for many years. But I've been her servant first, last, and always. And I've never lived a day, in good times or bad, that I didn't thank God for the privilege.

Long ago, something unusual happened to me that taught me the most valuable lesson of my life. I was blessed by misfortune. I mean that sincerely. I was blessed because

Greeting the Bush family at the Republican National Convention, St. Paul, Minnesota, September 4, 2008.

In this country, we believe everyone has something to contribute and deserves the opportunity to reach their God-given potential.

I served in the company of heroes and I witnessed a thousand acts of courage, and compassion, and love. On an October morning, in the Gulf of Tonkin, I prepared for my twenty-third mission over North Vietnam. I hadn't any worry I wouldn't come back safe and sound. I thought I was tougher than anyone.

I was pretty independent then, too.

I liked to bend a few rules and pick a few fights for the fun of it. But I did it for my own pleasure, my own pride. I didn't think there was a cause that was more important than me. Then I found myself falling toward the middle of a small lake in the city of Hanoi, with two broken arms, a broken leg, and an angry crowd waiting to greet me. I was dumped in a dark cell and left to die. I didn't feel so tough anymore.

When they discovered my father was an admiral, they took me to a hospital. They couldn't set my bones properly, so they just slapped a cast on me. And when I didn't get better and was down to about a hundred pounds, they put me in a cell with two other Americans. I couldn't do anything. I couldn't even feed myself. They did it for me. I was beginning to learn the limits of my selfish independence. Those men saved my life.

I was in solitary confinement when my captors offered to release me. I knew why. If I went home, they would use it as propaganda to demoralize my fellow prisoners. Our code said we could only go home in the order of our capture, and there were men who had been shot down long before me. I thought about it, though. I wasn't in great shape, and I missed everything about America, but I turned it down. A lot of prisoners had it much worse than I did. I'd been mistreated before, but not as badly as many others. I always liked to strut a little after I'd been roughed up to show the other guys I was tough enough to take it.

But after I turned down their offer, they worked me over harder than they ever had before, for a long time, and they broke me. When they brought me back to my cell, I was hurt and ashamed, and I didn't know how I could face my fellow prisoners. The good man in the cell next door to me, my friend, Bob Craner, saved me. Through taps on a wall, he told me I had fought as hard as I could. No man can always stand alone. And then he told me to get back up and fight again for my country and for the men I had the honor to serve with, because every day they fought for me.

I fell in love with my country when I was a prisoner in someone else's. I loved it not just for the many comforts of life here. I loved it for its decency, for its faith in the wisdom, justice, and goodness of its people. I loved it because it was not just a place, but an idea, a cause worth fighting for. I was never the same again; I wasn't my own man anymore; I was my country's.

I'm not running for president because I think I'm blessed with such personal greatness that history has anointed me to save our country in its hour of need. My country saved me, and I cannot forget it. And I will fight for her for as long as I draw breath, so help me God.

My friends, if you find faults with our country, make it a better one. If you're disappointed with the mistakes of government, join its ranks and work to correct them. Enlist in our Armed Forces. Become a teacher. Enter the ministry. Run for public office. Feed a hungry child. Teach an illiterate adult to read. Comfort the afflicted. Defend the rights of the oppressed. Our country will be the better, and you will be the happier, because nothing brings greater happiness in life than to serve a cause greater than yourself.

I'm going to fight for my cause every day as your president. I'm going to fight to make sure every American has every reason to thank God, as I thank him, that I'm an American, a proud citizen of the greatest country on Earth. And with hard work, strong faith, and a little courage, great things are always within our reach.

Fight with me. Fight with me.

Fight for what's right for our country. Fight for the ideals and character of a free people. Fight for our children's future. Fight for justice and opportunity for all. Stand up to defend our country from its enemies. Stand up for each other, for beautiful, blessed, bountiful America.

Stand up, stand up, stand up, and fight.

Nothing is inevitable here. We're Americans, and we never give up. We never quit. We never hide from history. We make history.

Thank you, and God bless you, and God bless America.

> My friends, if you find faults with our country, make it a better one. . . . Nothing brings greater happiness in life than to serve a cause greater than yourself.

(Following pages) Governor Palin and Senator McCain on the campaign trail at the Anoka County–Blaine Airport, September 2008.

"She knows where she comes from and she knows who she works for. She stands up for what's right, and she doesn't let anyone tell her to sit down."

—John McCain

(Previous pages) A campaign rally in Denver, Colorado, October 2008.

◄ McCain and Palin hug at a campaign rally in Blaine, Minnesota, September 2008.

▲ The presidential candidate asks his running mate what she ordered at Arthur Bryant's Barbeque in Kansas City, Missouri, September 7, 2008.

◀ Republican vice presidential candidate (and Alaska governor) Sarah Palin with her husband, Todd, and Cindy McCain during a campaign rally in Hershey, Pennsylvania, October 2008. ▲ Senator McCain, Todd and Sarah Palin, and Cindy McCain at an election night rally in Phoenix, November 4, 2008. (Following pages) Senator John McCain waiting for a flight to Chicago to meet with president-elect Barack Obama to discuss working together, November 16, 2008.

# PART FOUR

# STATESMAN

"We have to fight isolationism, protectionism, and nativism. We have to defeat those who would worsen our divisions. We have to remind our sons and daughters that we became the most powerful nation on earth by tearing down walls, not building them."

—John McCain

With his last campaign for president in the rearview and the acknowledgment that he would never hold the highest office in the land, McCain, as always, looked forward. He returned to the Senate determined to continue influencing US policy at home and abroad.

The fiery maverick became a dealmaker. In one especially important negotiation, McCain helped to stave off a political meltdown over Senate rules when he persuaded Democrats to leave the Senate filibuster rules alone and Republicans to confirm President Obama's nominees.

He worked with Democrats on immigration reform legislation, but that fell victim to politics and did not succeed.

Throughout the Obama presidency McCain was a critic but never a screed. He didn't buy into criticism of the president on false or personal grounds, only on his positions, particularly on policy involving the Middle East, and on what he saw as indecisiveness on the part of the president.

He was especially critical of the administration's handling of the attack on the US diplomatic compound in Benghazi, Libya. In his view, the Obama administration had not paid enough attention to the strength of Al-Qaeda-affiliated groups in the area, and that led to the attack and the deaths of four Americans.

(Previous pages) In the Russell Senate Office Building, 1996.

◀ Senators John McCain and Lindsey Graham in the US Capitol, December 2010.

McCain characterized administration policy on the Middle East as "weak," and he blamed President Obama for what he called a "feckless" foreign policy that allowed the Russians to send troops into Ukraine.

He held tight to his principles no matter who was in the Oval Office, though he was never mean-spirited about his criticism.

When McCain's son Jack (John S. McCain IV)—continuing the family's Navy tradition—graduated from the U.S. Naval Academy at Annapolis, President Obama was there to present the diploma.

McCain was a critic of the United States' use of torture and succeeded in passing an amendment to the National Defense Authorization Act that bans brutal interrogation techniques, including waterboarding. McCain's history of imprisonment and torture gave him special standing in the debate on the amendment and a platform from which to criticize then candidate Donald Trump, who took a pro-waterboarding stance during the 2016 presidential campaign.

McCain continued using his expertise in foreign affairs flying around the world to meet with foreign leaders and work with other governments. He was an opponent of Ukrainian president Viktor Yanukovych, and appeared in Kiev to tout that position. Following Yanukovych's overthrow, he supported providing arms to Ukrainian military forces. He even shared a delegation to Estonia with then senator Hillary Clinton, where the two bonded over vodka.

McCain had no love for President Trump, and their testy relationship was exacerbated when Trump downplayed McCain's hero status during the 2016 campaign: "I like heroes who weren't captured."

McCain shot back: "I've faced greater challenges than this."

In May 2017, McCain, in a tweet, called for a special congressional committee to investigate President Trump's 2016 campaign and whether it had a connection to Russian operatives.

When he was diagnosed with an aggressive form of brain cancer in 2017, McCain vowed to fight it with the same vigor with which he had overcome all of his many challenges through life.

The outpouring of sympathy and support that followed was led by President Obama who tweeted: "John McCain is an American hero & one of the bravest fighters I've ever known. Cancer doesn't know what it's up against."

The diagnosis liberated him, in a way. He voted against a bill that would have killed the Affordable Care Act, President Obama's signature healthcare law. His very visible thumbs-down gesture was captured on Senate cameras.

He gave a speech shortly before, urging the Senate he loved to return to the role it used to play in American government—that of a leader, negotiator, compromiser, and problem solver. "Let's trust each other," he said. "We've been spinning our wheels on too many important issues because we keep trying to find a way to win without help from across the aisle."

Barbara Bush, with John and CIndy McCain, 2008.

McCain was good friends with Senator Edward Kennedy, the liberal lion from Massachusetts, when they served in the Senate together. The two laughed together and legislated together. They passed the Patient's Bill of Rights together. In his eulogy in 2009 for Kennedy, McCain shared how he missed him every day.

McCain was diagnosed with the same type of brain cancer that felled Kennedy.

In light of the diagnosis, McCain was philosophical about the great and full life he has lived. He vowed to fight the cancer as he had every other obstacle in his life, but he was realistic about the odds. "I'm facing a challenge, but I've faced other challenges, and I'm confident about getting through this one as well."

He knew it was serious, however.

"Every life has to end one way or another," McCain said.

Those who know him say he never thinks much about the ending; he's too busy living life and grabbing it with both hands. Perhaps that's because he lost five and a half years to a prison cell, perhaps it is because of his family tradition of striving for success, but his style is always to keep moving, learning, and doing.

The tributes to him at that time came from the highest levels, both friends and adversaries: President Donald Trump, former Presidents George H.W. Bush, George W. Bush, Barack Obama, and former Vice President Joe Biden among them. The first President Bush, the eldest of the group, probably said it best:

"The Hanoi Hilton couldn't break John McCain's spirit many years ago, so Barbara and I know—with confidence—he and his family will meet this latest battle in his singular life of service, with courage and determination," he said in a statement.

No matter how it ends, McCain already has experienced much in his life—a son, survivor, spouse, senator, and statesman. Altogether, a "singular life of service" by a man who believes in his country and serves it to the best of his estimable ability.

President Obama congratulates graduate John Sidney McCain IV (Jack) after delivering the commencement address to the class of 2009 at the Naval Academy graduation and commissioning ceremony, May 22, 2009.

▲ President Reagan meeting with Republican Senate candidate
John McCain in the Oval Office, 1986. ▶ Senator McCain
at the Republican National Convention, 1988.

"In public life you not only have to be careful about what you do but you have to be careful about what you appear to do."

—John McCain

▲ Senator John McCain testifying before the Senate Ethics Committee about the Keating Five scandal, January 4, 1991.

▶ Facing reporters with his wife, Cindy, January 5, 1991.

▲ Flanked by reporters, John McCain walks back to the Capitol after a press conference on the McCain Bill, which took on the powerful tobacco industry, June 1998. ▶ After arriving in the early afternoon from a trip to Hawaii, in celebration of his eighteenth wedding anniversary, Commerce Committee staff director John Raidt gives the senator a briefing as he shaves. (Following pages) Senators Hillary Clinton and John McCain listen to President George W. Bush during the National Prayer Breakfast, 2007.

◀ Vice President Joe Biden administers the Senate oath of office during
a swearing-in ceremony reenactment, January 3, 2017. ▲ Representative
Rahm Emanuel, Representative Gil Gutknecht, Senator John McCain, Senator
Byron L Dorgan, and Representative Bernie Sanders during the Governors
Prescription Drug Summit, February 24, 2004.

"I enjoy my work and am grateful for the honor of serving in the United States Senate. There are many people in Congress . . . who are smarter, wiser, and more capable than I am. To be in their company is a privilege and a first-rate education. "

—John McCain

▲ John McCain heading to a GOP luncheon after he and Senator Feingold talked to reporters about their campaign finance bill, March 2001. ▶ Senator John McCain leaving his office in the Russell Building on Capitol Hill, March 2001.

"In the McCain-Feingold Bill, these two impressive senators insisted that it is time to close the most scandalous loopholes festering in our election laws, and end the corrosive and corrupting power of big money in federal elections."

—Senator Ted Kennedy

(Previous pages) During a news conference on the release of the
September 11 Commission report, July 2004. ◀ Calling in to staff
members to check on the status of amendments to his campaign finance
reform bill after addressing the students of his former high school
in Virginia, March 2001. ▲ With Senator Russ Feingold at a hearing
titled "Lobbying Reform: Proposals and Issues," January 2006.

◄ Meeting President George W. Bush for a private lunch at the White House to discuss his endorsement as the Republican presidential nominee in March 2008.
▲ Secretary of State Hillary Clinton and Senator John McCain during Senator John Kerry's Secretary of State confirmation hearing, January 24, 2013.

◀ At the VFW Sandy Coor Post 1433 in Glendale, Arizona, with Post Commander Dan Muller in 2010. ▲ With the families of flight 93 at the temporary memorial in Shanksville, Pennsylvania, September 11, 2008. (Following pages) Speaking at the Navy–Marine Corps Memorial Stadium, April 2, 2008.

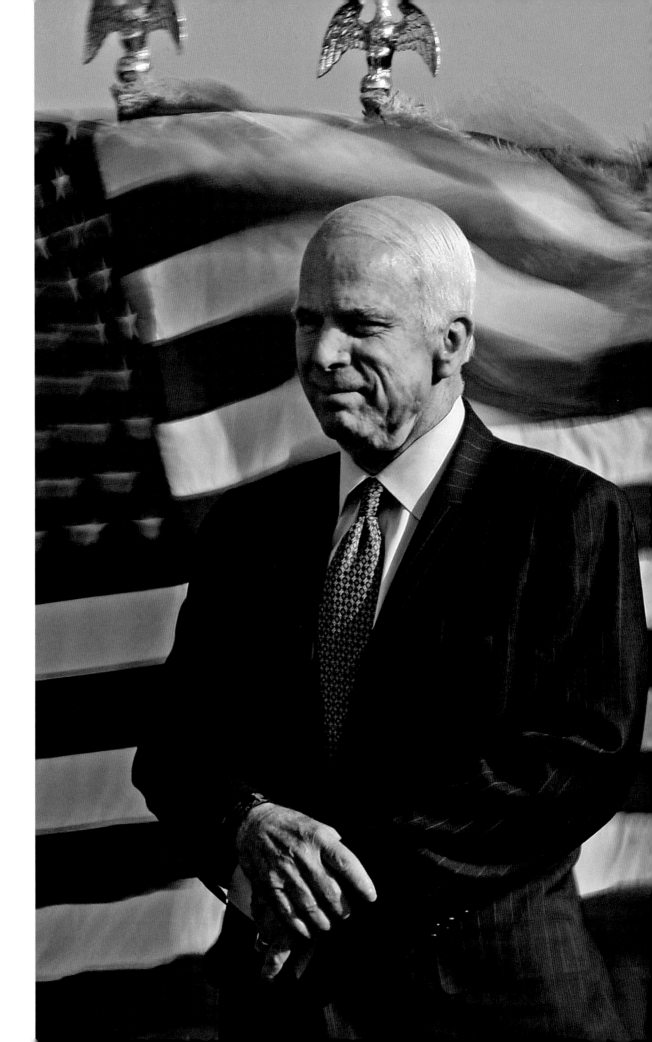

▲ Touring the ports of Long Beach and Los Angeles with California governor Arnold Schwarzenegger, 2007. ◀ With Australian prime minister Julia Gillard at an exhibition marking the sixtieth anniversary of the Australia, New Zealand, United States Security Treaty, 2011. ▶ With Britain's Prince Harry at an exhibit on landmines and unexploded ordnance on Capitol Hill, 2013.

▲ With President Ronald Reagan at the White House in 1986. ◀ With Senator Barack Obama at a hearing on lobbying reform in 2006. ▶ Walking to the Rose Garden with President Bill Clinton and Senator John Kerry to announce the signing of the Bilateral Trade Agreement with Vietnam, July 2000.

# JOHN MCCAIN ON KEY SENATE HEALTHCARE VOTE

The Senate Floor, Washington, DC
July 25, 2017

**I'VE STOOD IN THIS PLACE MANY TIMES** and addressed as president many presiding officers. I have been so addressed when I have sat in that chair, as close as I will ever be to a presidency.

It is an honorific we're almost indifferent to, isn't it. In truth, presiding over the Senate can be a nuisance, a bit of a ceremonial bore, and it is usually relegated to the more junior members of the majority.

But as I stand here today—looking a little worse for wear I'm sure—I have a refreshed appreciation for the protocols and customs of this body, and for the other ninety-nine privileged souls who have been elected to this Senate.

I have been a member of the United States Senate for thirty years. I had another long, if not as long, career before I arrived here, another profession that was profoundly rewarding, and in which I had experiences and friendships that I revere. But make no mistake, my service here is the most important job I have had in my life. And I am so grateful to the people of Arizona for the privilege—for the honor—of serving here and the opportunities it gives me to play a small role in the history of the country I love.

I've known and admired men and women in the Senate who played much more than a small role in our history, true statesmen, giants of American politics. They came from both parties, and from various backgrounds. Their ambitions were frequently in conflict. They held different views on the issues of the day. And they often had very serious disagreements about how best to serve the national interest.

But they knew that however sharp and heartfelt their disputes, however keen their ambitions, they had an obligation to work collaboratively to ensure the Senate discharged its constitutional responsibilities effectively. Our responsibilities are important, vitally important, to the continued success of our republic. And our arcane rules and customs are deliberately intended to require broad cooperation to function well at all. The most revered members

> And I am so grateful to the people of Arizona for the privilege—for the honor—of serving here . . .

of this institution accepted the necessity of compromise in order to make incremental progress on solving America's problems and to defend her from her adversaries.

That principled mindset and the service of our predecessors who possessed it come to mind when I hear the Senate referred to as the world's greatest deliberative body. I'm not sure we can claim that distinction with a straight face today. I'm sure it wasn't always deserved in previous eras, either. But I'm sure there have been times when it was, and I was privileged to witness some of those occasions.

Our deliberations today, not just our debates, but the exercise of all our responsibilities—authorizing government policies, appropriating the funds to implement them, exercising our advice and consent role—are often lively and interesting. They can be sincere and principled. But they are more partisan, more tribal more of the time than any other time I remember. Our deliberations can still be important and useful, but I think we'd all agree they haven't been overburdened by greatness lately. And right now they aren't producing much for the American people.

> Our deliberations can still be important and useful, but I think we'd all agree they haven't been overburdened by greatness lately.

Both sides have let this happen. Let's leave the history of who shot first to the historians. I suspect they'll find we all conspired in our decline—either by deliberate actions or neglect. We've all played some role in it. Certainly I have. Sometimes, I've let my passion rule my reason. Sometimes, I made it harder to find common ground because of something harsh I said to a colleague. Sometimes, I wanted to win more for the sake of winning than to achieve a contested policy.

Incremental progress, compromises that each side criticize but also accept, just plain muddling through to chip away at problems and keep our enemies from doing their worst isn't glamorous or exciting. It doesn't feel like a political triumph. But it's usually the most we can expect from our system of government, operating in a country as diverse and quarrelsome and free as ours.

Considering the injustice and cruelties inflicted by autocratic governments, and how corruptible human nature can be, the problem solving our system does make possible, the fitful progress it produces, and the liberty and justice it preserves is a magnificent achievement.

Our system doesn't depend on our nobility. It accounts for our imperfections, and gives an order to our individual strivings that has helped make ours the most powerful and prosperous society on earth. It is our responsibility to preserve that, even when it requires us to do something less satisfying than "winning." Even when we must give a little to get a little. Even when our efforts manage just three yards and a cloud of dust, while critics on both sides denounce us for timidity, for our failure to "triumph."

I hope we can again rely on humility, on our need to cooperate, on our dependence on each other to learn how to trust each other again and by so doing better serve the people who elected us. Stop listening to the bombastic loudmouths on the radio and television and the Internet. To hell with them. They don't want anything done for the public good. Our incapacity is their livelihood.

Stop listening to the bombastic loudmouths on the radio and television and the Internet.

Let's trust each other. Let's return to regular order. We've been spinning our wheels on too many important issues because we keep trying to find a way to win without help from across the aisle. That's an approach that's been employed by both sides, mandating legislation from the top down, without any support from the other side, with all the parliamentary maneuvers that requires.

We're getting nothing done. All we've really done this year is confirm Neil Gorsuch to the Supreme Court. Our healthcare insurance system is a mess. We all know it, those who support Obamacare and those who oppose it. Something has to be done. We Republicans have looked for a way to end it and replace it with something else without paying a terrible political price. We haven't found it yet, and I'm not sure we will. All we've managed to do is make more popular a policy that wasn't very popular when we started trying to get rid of it.

I voted for the motion to proceed to allow debate to continue and amendments to be offered. I will not vote for the bill as it is today. It's a shell of a bill right now. We all know that. I have changes urged by my state's governor that will have to be included to earn my support for final passage of any bill. I know many of you will have to see the bill changed substantially for you to support it.

We've tried to do this by coming up with a proposal behind closed doors in consultation with the administration, then springing it on skeptical members, trying to convince them it's better than nothing, asking us to swallow our doubts and force it past a unified opposition. I don't think that is going to work in the end. And it probably shouldn't.

The Obama administration and congressional Democrats shouldn't have forced through Congress without any opposition support a social and economic change as massive as Obamacare. And we shouldn't do the same with ours.

Why don't we try the old way of legislating in the Senate, the way our rules and customs encourage us to act. If this process ends in failure, which seem likely, then let's return to regular order.

Let the Health, Education, Labor, and Pensions Committee under Chairman Alexander and Ranking Member Murray hold hearings, try to report a bill out of committee with contributions from both sides. Then bring it to the floor for amendment and debate, and see if we can pass something that will be imperfect, full of compromises, and not very pleasing to implacable partisans on either side, but that might provide workable solutions to problems Americans are struggling with today.

What do we have to lose by trying to work together to find those solutions? We're not getting much done apart. I don't think any of us feel very proud of our incapacity. Merely preventing your political opponents from doing what they want isn't the most inspiring work. There's greater satisfaction in respecting our differences, but not letting them prevent agreements that don't require abandonment of core principles, agreements made in good faith that help improve lives and protect the American people.

The Senate is capable of that. We know that. We've seen it before. I've seen it happen many times. And the times when I was involved even in a modest way with working out a bipartisan response to a national problem or threat are the proudest moments of my career, and by far the most satisfying.

This place is important. The work we do is important. Our strange rules and seemingly eccentric practices that slow our proceedings and insist on our cooperation are important. Our founders envisioned the Senate as the more deliberative, careful body

Why don't we try the old way of legislating in the Senate ... What do we have to lose by trying to work together to find those solutions?

Our success in meeting all these awesome constitutional obligations depends on cooperation among ourselves. . . . We are the servants of a great nation.

that operates at a greater distance than the other body from the public passions of the hour.

We are an important check on the powers of the executive. Our consent is necessary for the president to appoint jurists and powerful government officials and in many respects to conduct foreign policy. Whether or not we are of the same party, we are not the president's subordinates. We are his equal!

As his responsibilities are onerous, many, and powerful, so are ours. And we play a vital role in shaping and directing the judiciary, the military, and the cabinet in planning and supporting foreign and domestic policies. Our success in meeting all these awesome constitutional obligations depends on cooperation among ourselves.

The success of the Senate is important to the continued success of America. This country—this big, boisterous, brawling, intemperate, restless, striving, daring, beautiful, bountiful, brave, good, and magnificent country—needs us to help it thrive. That responsibility is more important than any of our personal interests or political affiliations.

We are the servants of a great nation, a nation "conceived in liberty, and dedicated to the proposition that all men are created equal." More people have lived free and prosperous lives here than in any other nation. We have acquired unprecedented wealth and power because of our governing principles and because our government defended those principles.

America has made a greater contribution than any other nation to an international order that has liberated more people from tyranny and poverty than ever before in history. We have been the greatest example, the greatest supporter, and the greatest defender of that order. We aren't afraid. We don't covet other people's land and wealth. We don't hide behind walls. We breach them. We are a blessing to humanity.

What greater cause could we hope to serve than helping keep America the strong, aspiring, inspirational beacon of liberty and defender of the dignity of all human beings and their right to freedom and equal justice? That is the cause that binds us and is so much more powerful and worthy than the small differences that divide us.

What a great honor and extraordinary opportunity it is to serve in this body. It's a privilege to serve with all of you. I mean it. Many of you have reached out in the last few days with your concern and your prayers, and it means a lot to me. It really does. I've had so many people say such nice things about me recently that I think some of you must have me confused with someone else. I appreciate it though, every word, even if much of it isn't deserved.

I'll be here for a few days, I hope, managing the floor debate on the defense authorization bill, which, I'm proud to say is again a product of bipartisan cooperation and trust among the members of the Senate Armed Services Committee.

After that, I'm going home for a while to treat my illness. I have every intention of returning here and giving many of you cause to regret all the nice things you said about me. And, I hope, to impress on you again that it is an honor to serve the American people in your company.

Thank you, fellow senators.

On the Senate floor dramatically giving his "no" vote on repeal of portions of the Affordable Care Act in the early hours of July 28, 2017.

"He is loyal to his friends, he loves his country. If he has to stand up to his party for his country, so be it. He would die for this country. I love him to death."

—Senator Lindsey Graham

▲ Senators John McCain, Charles Schumer, and Lindsey Graham before President Barack Obama's State of the Union address, February 12, 2013. ▶ On Capitol Hill with New York senator Charles Schumer in 2015.

"Ultimately, freedom of information is critical for a democracy to succeed. We become better, stronger, and more effective societies by having an informed and engaged public that pushes policymakers to best represent not only our interests but also our values. Journalists play a major role in the promotion and protection of democracy and our unalienable rights, and they must be able to do their jobs freely. Only truth and transparency can guarantee freedom."

—John McCain

With reporters on Capitol Hill after the Senate
voted to pass debt legislation in August 2011.

▲ United States Senate Armed Services Committee members (from left) Senators Ted Kennedy, Joe Lieberman, John McCain, and John Warner prior to a hearing on the situation in Iraq, April 8, 2008.

▲ (Clockwise from top left) Former national security advisor Sandy Berger, Senator John McCain, Representative Eliot Engel, former secretary of state Condoleezza Rice, former national security advisor Brent Scowcroft, former homeland security advisor Frances Townsend, Secretary of State John Kerry, former State Department chief of staff and director of policy planning Jon Finer, former secretary of state James Baker, and former national security advisor Stephen Hadley discuss foreign policy challenges as they return from the funeral of King Abdullah of Saudi Arabia in January 2015.

(Previous pages) With fellow former Vietnam prisoners of war honoring one of their own, retired vice admiral William P. Lawrence, at his funeral in 2005. ◀ Senator McCain promoting Marine Staff Sergeant Antonio Aburto during a ceremony at Camp Eggers, Kabul, Afghanistan, in 2010. ▲ Senate Armed Services committee chairman McCain comforting Victor Sibayan, whose son, Navy FC1(SW) Carlos Sibayan, died in the USS *Fitzgerald* collision in 2017.

# JOHN MCCAIN'S REMARKS UPON BEING AWARDED THE NATIONAL CONSTITUTION CENTER'S LIBERTY MEDAL [abridged]

National Constitution Center, Philadelphia, Pennsylvania
October 16, 2017

VICE PRESIDENT BIDEN AND I have known each other for a lot of years now, more than forty, if you're counting. We knew each other back when we were young and handsome and smarter than everyone else but were too modest to say so.

Joe was already a senator, and I was the Navy's liaison to the Senate. My duties included escorting Senate delegations on overseas trips, and in that capacity, I supervised the disposition of the delegation's luggage, which could require—now and again when no one of lower rank was available for the job—that I carry someone worthy's bag. Once or twice that worthy turned out to be the young senator from Delaware. I've resented it ever since.

Joe has heard me joke about that before. I hope he has heard, too, my profession of gratitude for his friendship these many years. It has meant a lot to me. We served in the Senate together for over twenty years, during some eventful times, as we passed from young men to the fossils who appear before you this evening.

We didn't always agree on the issues. We often argued—sometimes passionately. But we believed in each other's patriotism and the sincerity of each other's convictions. We believed in the institution we were privileged to serve in. We believed in our mutual responsibility to help make the place work and to cooperate in finding solutions to our country's problems. We believed in our country and in our country's indispensability to international peace and stability and to the progress of humanity. And through it all, whether we argued or agreed, Joe was good company.

Thank you, old friend, for your company and your service to America. . . .

Some years ago, I was present at an event where an earlier Liberty Medal recipient spoke about America's values and the sacrifices made for them. It was 1991, and I was attending the ceremony commemorating the fiftieth anniversary of the attack on Pearl Harbor. The World War II veteran, estimable patriot and good man, President George H. W. Bush, gave a moving speech at the USS *Arizona* memorial. I remember it very well. His voice was thick with emotion as he neared the end of his address.

John McCain upon recieving the 2017 Liberty Medal.

I imagine he was thinking not only of the brave Americans who lost their lives on December 7, 1941, but of the friends he had served with and lost in the Pacific, where he had been the Navy's youngest aviator. "Look at the water here, clear and quiet . . ." he directed. "One day, in what now seems another lifetime, it wrapped its arms around the finest sons any nation could ever have, and it carried them to a better world." He could barely get out the last line: "May God bless them, and may God bless America, the most wondrous land on earth."

The most wondrous land on earth, indeed. I've had the good fortune to spend sixty years in service to this wondrous land. It has not been perfect service, to be sure, and there were probably times when the country might have benefited from a little less of my help. But I've tried to deserve the privilege as best I can, and I've been repaid a thousand times over with adventures, with good company, and with the satisfaction of serving something more important than myself, of being a bit player in the extraordinary story of America. And I am so very grateful.

What a privilege it is to serve this big, boisterous, brawling, intemperate, striving, daring, beautiful, bountiful, brave, magnificent country. With all our flaws, all our mistakes, with all the frailties of human nature as much on display as our virtues, with all the rancor and anger of our politics, we are blessed.

We are living in the land of the free, the land where anything is possible, the land of the immigrant's dream, the land with the storied past forgotten in the rush to the imagined future, the land that repairs and reinvents itself, the land where a person can escape the consequences of a self-centered youth and know the satisfaction of sacrificing for an ideal, the land where you can go from aimless rebellion to a noble cause, and from the bottom of your class to your party's nomination for president.

We are blessed, and we have been a blessing to humanity in turn.

The international order we helped build from the ashes of world war, and that we defend to this day, has liberated more people from tyranny and poverty than ever before in history. This wondrous land has shared its treasures and ideals and shed the blood of its finest patriots to help make another, better world. And as we did so, we made our own civilization more just, freer, more accomplished and prosperous than the America that existed when I watched my father go off to war on December 7, 1941.

To fear the world we have organized and led for three-quarters of a century, to abandon the ideals we have advanced around the globe, to refuse the obligations of international leadership and our duty to remain "the last best hope of earth" for the sake of some half-baked, spurious nationalism cooked up by people who would rather find scapegoats than solve problems is as unpatriotic as an attachment to any other tired dogma of the past that Americans consigned to the ash heap of history.

We live in a land made of ideals, not blood and soil. We are the custodians of those ideals at home and their champion abroad. We have done great good in the world. That leadership has had its costs, but we have become incomparably powerful and wealthy as we did. We have a moral obligation to continue in our just cause, and we would bring more than shame on ourselves if we don't. We will not thrive in a world where our leadership and ideals are absent. We wouldn't deserve to.

I am the luckiest guy on earth. I have served America's cause—the cause of our security and the security of our friends, the cause of freedom and equal justice—all my adult life. I haven't always served it well. I haven't even always appreciated what I was serving. But among the few compensations of old age is the acuity of hindsight. I see now that I was part of something important that drew me along in its wake even when I was diverted by other interests. I was, knowingly or not, along for the ride as America made the future better than the past.

> I was, knowingly or not, along for the ride as America made the future better than the past.

And I have enjoyed it, every single day of it, the good ones and the not so good ones. I've been inspired by the service of better patriots than me. I've seen Americans make sacrifices for our country and her causes and for people who were strangers to them but for our common humanity, sacrifices that were much harder than the service asked of me. And I've seen the good they have done, the lives they freed from tyranny and injustice, the hope they encouraged, the dreams they made achievable.

May God bless them. May God bless America, and give us the strength and wisdom, the generosity and compassion, to do our duty for this wondrous land, and for the world that counts on us. With all its suffering and dangers, the world still looks to the example and leadership of America to become another, better place.

What greater cause could anyone ever serve.

Thank you again for this honor. I'll treasure it.

(Previous pages) President-elect Barack Obama giving a hand to the Republican presidential nominee at a dinner honoring McCain, January 19, 2009. ▲ Senator John McCain speaking to reporters on Capitol Hill, August 2, 2011. ▶ Photographed in Washington, DC, 2005.

> "I don't mind a good fight. For reasons known only to God, I've had quite a few tough ones in my life. But I learned an important lesson along the way: In the end, it matters less that you can fight. What you fight for is the real test."
>
> —John McCain

Senator John McCain walking down a hallway in his home surrounded by photographs and news clippings of his career, 2008.

# ACKNOWLEDGMENTS

The book is the work of an amazing team. Thanks to Esther Margolis of Newmarket Publishing Management for bringing me into her fold. She is a determined and estimable force with a wealth of information and savvy. Christopher Measom, of Night & Day Design, is a photo editor extraordinaire who managed to find and secure the perfect pictures, while keeping me and the project organized and on track. Timothy Shaner, also of Night & Day Design, beautifully designed the book to be easy on the eyes; it will be read again and again. Sterling Publishing executive editor Barbara Berger's overarching vision as well as her sharp eye and pen were invaluable. Also at Sterling, I am grateful to Chris Thompson, senior art director, interiors, for his insightful direction; and also to Elizabeth Lindy, senior art director, covers and cover designer, for the beautiful jacket design. We would also like to thank Rachel Cunningham for her quick, on-the-ground-in-Hanoi research; Dave Colamaria, the photo archivist at the Naval History and Heritage Command; and Claude Berube at the US Naval Academy Museum.

It's an honor to share in this book with legendary documentary filmmaker Ken Burns, who is as good with words as he is with images. I am also deeply indebted to those who wrote of McCain's life before, not the least of whom is the man himself and his singularly talented coauthor, Mark Salter. McCain's life story would make good fiction, but it is a better tale because it's real.

Thanks to Mom and Dad, who, though they may have disagreed with John McCain sometimes, were proud to pose with a candidate who respected journalism and journalists (especially their daughter). I am grateful to my husband, Ron Dziengiel, for his loving, steadfast encouragement of my work on this project. The "kids"—Kenny Dziengiel; Mark Dziengiel and Katie Machiz; and Charlotte Alaina "Charlie" Dziengiel—remind me daily that the future is in good hands and that John McCain's challenge to aspire to "something greater than our own self-interest" is on the way to being fulfilled.

—Elaine S. Povich, 2018

John McCain with the author, right, and her parents,
Don and Janice Povich, Portland, Maine, 2000 campaign.

# NOTES

## INTRODUCTION: ONE HELL OF A RIDE

**Page 1:** **"lightning in a bottle"**: "McCain Rolls into Philadelphia aboard Campaign Bus," CNN/AllPolitics, July 29, 2000. **"born to privilege"**: John McCain and Mark Salter, *Faith of My Fathers* (New York: Random House, 1999), 51. **"intercepted a Soviet-made surface-to-air missile"**: Elaine S. Povich, *John McCain: A Biography*, (Westport, CT: Greenwood Press, 2009), xv.

**Page 2:** **"reporters . . . 'my base'"**: Elaine S. Povich, *John McCain: A Biography* (Westport, CT: Greenwood Press, 2009), 118.

**Page 3:** **"Roberta Wright McCain who ran off"**: John McCain and Mark Salter, *Faith of My Fathers* (New York: Random House, 1999), 48.

**Page 4:** **"Too much had happened"**: John McCain and Mark Salter, *Worth the Fighting For: A Memoir*, (New York: Random House, 2002), 12. **"marriage to Cindy"**: Ibid., 32.

## PART ONE: NAVY SON & FAMILY MAN

**Page 9:** **"My grandfather was"**: John McCain and Mark Salter, *Faith of My Fathers* (New York: Random House, 1999), 7. **"December 7, 1941"**: Ibid., 79.

**Page 10:** **"'rock, paper, scissors'"**: John McCain and Mark Salter, *Faith of My Fathers* (New York: Random House, 1999), 147. **"Brazilian model"**: Ibid., 139. **"Marie, the Flame"**: Ibid., 154.

**Page 11:** **"USS *Forrestal* . . . horrific 1967 fire"**: R. W. Apple Jr., "Adm. McCain's Son, Forrestal Survivor, Is Missing in Raid," *New York Times* (October 28, 1967), 1. **"surface-to-air missiles were thick"**: Elaine S. Povich, *John McCain: A Biography* (Westport, CT: Greenwood Press, 2009), 30.

**Page 13:** **"He may have broken"**: Paul Alexander, *The Life of John McCain* (Hoboken, NJ: John Wiley and Sons, 2003), 25.

**Page 14:** **"I liked the squadron life"**: Carl Bernstein, "Nothing Left to Fear," *Vanity Fair*, December 1999.

**Page 18:** **"In Tokyo Harbor"**: "Senator McCain's Address to the Republican National Convention," First Union Center, Philadelphia, Pennsylvania, August 1, 2000.

**Page 30:** **"In the absolute end"**: "Candidates Wives Share Stage, Stories," CBS News, October 24, 2007, https://www.cbsnews.com/news/candidates-wives-share-stage-stories

## PART TWO: PRISONER OF WAR

**Page 35:** **"There is no way I can describe"**: John McCain, "John McCain, Prisoner of War: A First-Person Account," *US News and World Report*, May 14, 1973. **"French film crew"**: John McCain and Mark Salter, *Faith of My Fathers* (New York: Random House, 1999), 197.

**Page 36:** **"tapping code"**: John McCain and Mark Salter, *Faith of My Fathers* (New York: Random House, 1999), 211–212. **"Every man has a breaking point"**: John McCain, "John McCain, Prisoner of War: A First-Person Account," *US News and World Report*, May 14, 1973.

**Page 37:** **"McCain was released"**: John McCain, "A Former POW on Vietnam, Four Decades Later," *Wall Street Journal*, March 14, 2013.

**Page 38:** **"I hit the water and sank"**: John McCain, "John McCain, Prisoner of War: A First-Person Account," *US News and World Report*, May 14, 1973.

**Page 40:** **"I knew there was that anti-war element"**: Carl Bernstein, "Nothing Left to Fear," *Vanity Fair*, December 1999.

**Page 42:** **"I fell in love with my country"**: "Presidential Nomination Acceptance Speech," Republican National Convention, St. Paul, Minnesota, September 4, 2008.

**Page 49:** **"My marriage's collapse"**: John McCain and Mark Salter, *Worth the Fighting For: A Memoir* (New York: Random House, 2002), 13–14.

**Page 52:** **"It doesn't matter"**: James Carroll, "A Friendship That Ended the War," *New Yorker*, October 21, 1996.

## PART THREE: STRAIGHT TALK EXPRESS

**Page 63:** **"Make no mistake"**: "McCain's Impassioned Speech as He Returns to the Senate," *Washington Examiner,* July 25, 2017. **"leave the Navy"**: John McCain and Mark Salter, *Worth the Fighting For: A Memoir* (New York: Random House, 2002), 11. **"my marriage's collapse"**: Ibid., 32. **"lied about the seventeen-year difference"**: *The Tonight Show with Jay Leno*, NBC, May 5, 2008. http://youtube.com/watch?v=Hv7LUT1ezm0

**Page 64:** **"carpetbagger"**: Elaine S. Povich, *John McCain: A Biography* (Westport, CT: Greenwood Press, 2009), 64.

**Page 65:** **"being in a North Vietnamese prison"**: Elaine S. Povich, *John McCain: A Biography* (Westport, CT: Greenwood Press, 2009), 91. **"He won the New Hampshire primary"**: Elaine S. Povich, "Campaign 2000/Out of the Running/McCain Ends on a Quiet Note—But Doesn't Endorse Bush," *Newsday*, March 10, 2000. **"appetite had been whetted"**: Elaine S. Povich, *John McCain: A Biography*, (Westport, CT: Greenwood Press, 2009), 133. **"I wish Godspeed"**: CNN, "Transcript: McCain Concedes Presidency," November 4, 2008, http://edition.cnn.com/2008/POLITICS/11/04/mccain.transcript/index.html

**Page 75:** **"I ribbed aides"**: John McCain and Mark Salter, *Worth the Fighting For: A Memoir* (New York: Random House, 2002), 371.

**Page 86:** **"When the pundits"**: "John McCain's New Hampshire Primary Speech," *New York Times,* January 8, 2008.

**Page 98:** **"I am proud of my record"**: "Republican Debate in Simi Valley, Calif.," *New York Times*, January 30, 2008.

**Page 105:** **"There were many"**: Campaign speech at Faneuil Hall in Boston, February 4, 2008, video, CSPAN, https://www.c-span.org/video/?203984-1/mccain-campaign-event&start=1651

**Page 108:** **"Reporters became"**: John McCain and Mark Salter, *Worth the Fighting For: A Memoir* (New York: Random House, 2002), 370.

**Page 116:** **"It's a long way"**: "Palin's Speech at the Republican National Convention," *New York Times*, September 3, 2008.

**Page 119:** **"I hit a home run"**: Cindy McCain, "Speech to the Republican Convention," September 4, 2008, video, CSPAN, https://www.c-span.org/video/?280797-13/cindy-mccain-2008-convention-speech

**Page 133:** **"She knows where"**: "McCain's acceptance speech," *Politico*, September 4, 2008.

# NOTES

**PART FOUR: STATESMAN**

**Page 141: "We have to fight isolationism"**: "McCain Remarks to Brigade of Midshipmen at U.S. Naval Academy," Annapolis, Maryland, October 30, 2017. **"filibuster rules"**: Lisa Mascaro and Michael Memoli, "Schumer McCain, Team up for Senate Filibuster Deal," *Los Angeles Times,* July 16, 2013. **"critic never a screed"**: "McCain gives Obama an 'F' on foreign policy," *The Hill*, February 10, 2016, http://thehill.com/video/in-the-news/268912-mccain-obama-deserves-an-f-on-foreign-policy.

**Page 142: "'feckless' foreign policy"**: Jake Miller, "John McCain Blames Obama's 'Feckless' Foreign Policy for Ukraine Crisis," *CBS News*, March 3, 2014. **"Jack . . . graduated"**: "At Naval Academy Graduation, Lives of McCain, Obama, Overlap," CNN, May 22, 2009, http://www.cnn.com/2009/POLITICS/05/22/obama.mccain/index.html. **"bans brutal interrogation"**: "Senate Passes McCain Anti-Torture Amendment," Azcentral.com, June 17, 2015. **"opponent of Ukrainian President Viktor Yanukovych"**: "McCain to Lead Delegation to Ukraine," *Daily Beast,* March 12, 2014. **"heroes who weren't captured"**: Ben Schreckinger, "Trump Attacks McCain: 'I Like Heroes Who Weren't Captured,'" *Politico,* July 18, 2015. **"I've faced greater"**: Chris Perez, "McCain Takes Veiled Shot at Trump," *New York Post*, October 23, 2017.

**Page 143: "When he was diagnosed"**: Paul Kane, "John McCain, Republican Senator from Arizona, Diagnosed with Brain Tumor," *Washington Post,* July 19, 2017. **"Let's trust each other"**: "Full Text of John McCain's Senate Floor Speech: 'Let's Return to Regular Order,'" *USA Today*, July 25, 2017.

**Page 145: "Every life has to end"**: *State of the Union with Jake Tapper*, CNN, September 10, 2017. http://www.cnn.com/videos/politics/2017/09/10/sotu-mccain-every-life.cnn **"The Hanoi Hilton couldn't break"**: "Lawmakers Send Well Wishes to John McCain following Brain Tumor Announcement," ABC News, July 19, 2017. http://abcnews.go.com/Politics/lawmakers-send-wishes-john-mccain-brain-tumor-announcement/story?id=48736469

**Page 148: "In public life"**: Helen Dewar, "'Keating Five' Senators Begin Final Defense," *Washington Post*, January 5, 1991.

**Page 156: "I enjoy my work"**: John McCain and Mark Salter, *Worth the Fighting For: A Memoir* (New York: Random House, 2002), xv.

**Page 160: "In the McCain-Feingold Bill"**: "Remarks of Senator Edward M. Kennedy on the presentation of the 1999 Profile in Courage Award to Senator John McCain and Senator Russell Feingold," May 24, 1999, https://www.jfklibrary.org/Events-and-Awards/Profile-in-Courage-Award/Award-Recipients/John-McCain-1999.aspx?t=5

**Page 178: "He is loyal"**: Eric Bradner, "John McCain, Lindsey Graham Get Emotional Describing Friendship: 'I Love Him to Death'" CNN, March 1, 2017, http://www.cnn.com/2017/03/01/politics/john-mccain-lindsey-graham-emotional/index.html

**Page 181: "Ultimately, freedom of"**: John McCain, "Mr. President, stop attacking the press," *Washington Post*, January 16, 2018.

**Page 196: "I don't mind"**: John McCain, "Address Accepting the Presidential Nomination at the Republican National Convention in Saint Paul,"September 4, 2008, American Presidency Project, http://www.presidency.ucsb.edu/ws/index.php?pid=78576

# PICTURE CREDITS

**ALAMY**: 13 top: dpa picture alliance; 17: Everett Collection Historical; 35: Peter Treanor; 37: Everett Collection Inc.; 78: Aurora Photos; 79: Scott Goldsmith/Aurora Photos; 99: Andy Holzman/ZUMA Press; 128–129: Elizabeth Flores/*Star Tribune*/ZUMA Press; 136–137: dpa picture alliance archive; 140: ZUMA Press; 156, 158–159: Scott J. Ferrell/*Congressional Quarterly*; 162: Chip Somodevilla CNP/MediaPunch Inc.; 169: Michael Reynolds/Consolidated News Photos; 178: Charles Dharapak/Consolidated News Photos; 182: Ron Sachs/Consolidated News Photos; 183: US State Department; 186: Staff Sgt. Sarah Brown/PJF Military Collection; 192–193: Joshua Roberts/Consolidated News Photos.

**AP IMAGES**: ii: Stephan Savoia; 7; 8; 16; 22–23: Jim Cole; 26; 28 top: Dean Cox; 34: Horst Faas; 39 top; 48; 49 top: Dang van Phuoc; 52–53: John Duricka; 58: J. Scott Applewhite; 61: Stephan Savoia; 62: Larry Downing; 84–85: Alex Brandon; 97 top: Stephan Savoia; 97 bottom; 102: Jim Cole; 106–107: Matthew Putney; 109: Jim Cole; 111: Carolyn Kaster; 117: Charlie Neibergall; 130–131, 132, 133, 134, 135: Stephan Savoia; 147: Ron Edmonds; 148, 149: John Duricka; 154: Kevin Wolf; 157, 160: Stephan Savoia; 161: *CQ Roll Call*; 165: Stephan Savoia; 168 top: Kevin Chang; 170 bottom: *CQ Roll Call*; 179: Carolyn Kaster; 180–181, 187, 194: Jacquelyn Martin; 195: © RTPearson/MediaPunch/IPx; 196: Stephan Savoia.

**FREEPIK**: natanaelginting (part openers background).

**GETTY IMAGES**: viii: Jeff Riedel/Contour; 5: David Hume Kennerly; 10, 12: Terry Ashe/The LIFE Images Collection; 20: Alex Wong; 21: Chuck Kennedy/MCT; 24: Cynthia Johnson/The LIFE Images Collection; 25: Laura Patterson/*CQ Roll Call*; 27: Karin Cooper; 28 bottom: Paul Morigi/WireImage; 29: Ramin Talaie/Corbis; 30–31: Daivd Hume Kennerly; 39 bottom: AFP; 40, 41: Rolls Press/Popperfoto; 44, 46: Bettmann; 47; 50 top: CBS Photo Archive; 50 bottom, 51: Hoang Dinh Nam/AFP; 57: Stan Honda/AFP; 66 top: Harry Hamburg/NY Daily News Archive;

66 bottom: Mike Fiala/AFP; 67: Carolyn Cole/*Los Angeles Times*; 68–69: Harry Hamburg/NY Daily News Archive; 70: David Hume Kennerly; 71 top: Paul J. Richards/AFP; 71 bottom: John Gaps III/AFP; 72: Harry Hamburg/NY Daily News Archive; 73: Karin Cooper/Liaison; 74–75, 76–77, 82–83: David Hume Kennerly; 86–87: Jay L. Clendenin/*Los Angeles Times*; 89, 92: David Hume Kennerly; 94: Robyn Beck/AFP; 95: Chip Somodevilla; 96: John Moore; 98: Jim Watson/AFP; 99 top: Scott Olson; 100–101, 103, 104, 105, 108, 110: David Hume Kennerly; 112–113: Chip Somodevilla; 114: David Hume Kennerly; 115: Chip Somodevilla; 139: Ted Thai/The LIFE Picture Collection; 143: Dave Einsel; 144: Alex Wong; 150: Douglas Graham/*Congressional Quarterly*; 151: Scott J. Ferrell/*Congressional Quarterly*; 152–153: Brendan Smialowski/AFP; 163: Saul Loeb/AFP; 164: Paul J. Richards/AFP; 166–167: Mark Wilson; 168 bottom: Nicholas Kamm/AFP; 171: Stephen Jaffe/AFP; 189: William Thomas Cain.

**LIBRARY OF CONGRESS, PRINTS & PHOTOGRAPHS DIVISION:**
42–43: Thomas J. O'Halloran (LC-U9-27595) ; 118, 119, 121, 125, 170 top: The Carol M. Highsmith Archive.

**NATIONAL ARCHIVES AND RECORDS ADMINISTRATION**: 18: ID no. 6482830; 33: ID no. 1633553; 45: ID no. 66394362.

**NAVAL HISTORY AND HERITAGE COMMAND, PHOTO ARCHIVES:**
14 top: 80-G-469006; 14 bottom: 1112855; 15: L38-57.01.01; 19: NH 92607.

**ELAINE S. POVICH**: 198.

**THE RONALD REAGAN LIBRARY**: 49 bottom; 146.

**SETH POPPEL/YEARBOOK LIBRARY**: 13 bottom.

**US NAVY**: 184–185: Ken Mierzejewski.